TRAVELLERS

SHANGHAI
& SOUTHERN CHINA
including HONG KONG

By
GEORGE McDONALD

Written by George McDonald, updated by Peter Holmshaw
Original photography by Alex Kovprianoff and David Henley/CPA Media

Published by Thomas Cook Publishing
A division of Thomas Cook Tour Operations Limited
Company registration no 1450464 England
The Thomas Cook Business Park, Unit 9 Coningsby Road,
Peterborough PE3 8SB, United Kingdom
Email: books@thomascook.com, Tel: + 44 (0) 1733 416477
www.thomascookpublishing.com

Produced by Cambridge Publishing Management Limited
Burr Elm Court, Main Street, Caldecote CB23 7NU

ISBN: 978-1-84157-945-0

© 2002, 2004, 2006 Thomas Cook Publishing
This fourth edition © 2008
Text © Thomas Cook Publishing
Maps © Thomas Cook Publishing/PCGraphics (UK) Limited

Series Editor: Maisie Fitzpatrick
Production/DTP: Steven Collins

Printed and bound in Italy by Printer Trento

Cover photography: Back L–R: © Mehlig Manfred/SIME-4Corners Images;
© Romiti Fabrizio/SIME-4Corners Images. Front L–R: © Romiti
Fabrizio/SIME-4Corners Images; © Pignatelli Massimo/SIME-4Corners
Images; © Harald Sund/The Image Bank/Getty Images

The paper used for this book has been independently certified as having
been sourced from well-managed forests and recycled wood or fibre
according to the rules of the Forest Stewardship Council.
This book has been printed and bound in Italy by Printer Trento S.r.l.,
an FSC certified company for printing books on FSC mixed paper in
compliance with the chain of custody and on products labelling standards.

FSC
Mixed Sources
Product group from well-managed
forests and recycled wood or fibre

Cert no. CQ-COC-000012
www.fsc.org
© 1996 Forest Stewardship Council

Contents

Introduction

China is far too vast and diverse a country to encapsulate in a few words, leaving both writers and visitors mumbling truisms such as 'fascinating' and 'mysterious'. Imperial China, Communist China, today's China, rural China, urban China, the China of your preconceptions, the China of slick government propaganda – the traveller will meet a dizzying blend of all these and more in anything other than a brief visit to this country.

Add to this mixture the current frenzied development and it can all seem a little overwhelming. Nonetheless, travelling through China is bound to be an unforgettable experience. The country has the largest population on earth, a 5,000-year-old culture, a language spoken by one-fifth of humanity, and a deep desire to be counted among the ranks of the advanced nations. Despite this, China, particularly outside the big cities, makes few concessions (and often little sense) to foreign visitors.

While China's north is the historical and cultural homeland of the Han Chinese people, the south of the country represents its more recent and softer face. Abundant rainfall is ideal for rice cultivation and the seas provide bounty as well. Its warm and fertile lands attracted the Han – certainly more so than the frigid steppes north of them, populated by fierce nomadic tribes. Beginning with the Song Dynasty (960–1279), the Han gradually settled in the area, bringing Chinese culture but also absorbing the traditions of the indigenous people. As the Yellow River provided sustenance and transportation for the north, the longer and more powerful Yangzi River gave rise to great capitals such as Nanjing in the south.

Rewarding as China undoubtedly is, it is still a developing country. The pollution in cities and the poverty that still prevails in many rural areas contrast with breathtaking scenes of natural and man-made beauty. Many of China's best-known sights have been degraded by over-development. Fortunately, improved infrastructure and well-executed restorations have widened the number of historical sights that are accessible and well worth a visit.

Environmental degradation (*see pp92–3*) is also a serious issue for both the visitor and the Chinese people. Many Chinese cities are enshrouded in a permanent veil of air pollution, which is not only unattractive but a health concern, even for short-term visitors –

nothing can dim an ardour for exploration like a nasty cough. Although the central government is taking steps to address this problem (for example, in 2007 Huang Shan, one of China's most beautiful mountains, was closed to visitors for a three-year period to allow the flora and fauna to recuperate), conservation and rapid development do not go hand in hand, and much remains to be done.

When, in the early 1980s, China allowed foreigners to visit for the first time since the 1949 Communist revolution, visitors were often shocked by the lack of connection that China and its people had with the rest of the world. Empty store shelves, a uniformly drab and impoverished population and few restaurants worthy of the name all sent visitors scurrying home. How times have changed.

Shanghai now has lodgings, restaurants and shopping to rival, if not exceed, the standards of Western cities. Still, China remains a land of contrasts. Futuristic architecture and the latest fashions compete with the more traditional sights people come to see. China has the world's highest foreign exchange reserves and an economy bigger than Britain's, but peasants still plough their fields with water buffalo.

Possibly even more than most destinations, a visit to China requires an open frame of mind and a willingness to accept things as they are if you are to gain the insights that make the effort worthwhile. Travelling in China gives visitors a chance to try to unravel some of the strands in the ancient and modern Chinese puzzles, and to have some fun along the way.

Shanghai skyline at night

The land

The foremost city of the area covered in this guide is doubtlessly Shanghai. It is a city without a long history, but a colourful one to be sure. However, the attractive cities of Suzhou, Hangzhou, Nanjing and Yangzhou, and the islands of Hong Kong and Macao also offer good reasons to visit. Further afield, the tropical climate of the coastal provinces and the natural beauties of the more remote provinces of Yunnan or Tibet will show another facet of this complex country.

After the end of the first Opium War in 1842, The Treaty of Nanjing opened five 'treaty ports', including Shanghai, to foreign trade. Shanghai became a cosmopolitan city, referred to as the 'Paris of the Orient'. Those days ended abruptly in 1949, but today Shanghai has regained its verve and has not only futuristic architecture and world-class modern amenities, but an energy that one finds nowhere else in China or, arguably, on the planet. Hotels, restaurants, museums and sporting events all abound here, but fortunately the architecture of the former French Concession and the stately banks on the Bund serve as a reminder of Shanghai's past.

Within 200km (124 miles) of Shanghai, the historically important towns of Suzhou, Hangzhou, Nanjing and Yangzhou present splendid traditional architecture complemented by willow-lined lakes and canals.

Heading into true South China, the climate warms and the land becomes even more fertile in the coastal provinces of Fujian and Guangdong. Guangdong, adjacent to the Hong Kong Special Administrative Region, is where China's recent drive to modernisation began in the 1980s and continues today, with many rice fields now replaced by factories. The Hong Kong and Macao SAR's former British and Portuguese colonies are now politically part of China, but little else has changed. Hong Kong prospers through commerce and Macao through gambling.

The southwest provinces of Guizhou and Yunnan as well as the Autonomous Region of Guangxi are home to the country's most numerous and colourful ethnic minorities. North of Yunnan, Sichuan offers sacred mountains, a world-famous cuisine, and the starting point for cruises down the Yangzi River.

Further west, the Autonomous Region of Tibet is home to an ancient culture defined by the people's unshakable devotion to their fascinating religious beliefs.

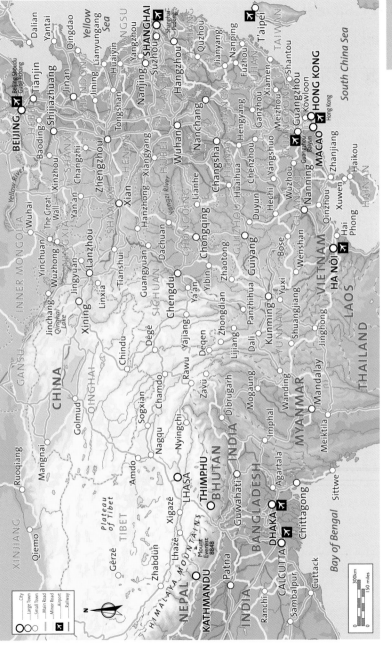

History

Circa 2000 BC Yangshao and Longshan cultures give rise to the Xia Dynasty, the first of the Chinese dynasties. Fine pottery produced.

1766– 1122 BC Shang Dynasty. Capital at Anyang, in present-day Henan Province. Jade and bronze decorative items are made.

1122– 256 BC Zhou Dynasty. Confucius formulates his code of ethics, Sun Tzu writes *The Art of War*, and the first Taoist texts are written.

221– 206 BC Qin Dynasty. Emperor Qin Shi Huang Di unites China. Chang'an (present-day Xian) is established as the capital. Weights, measures and currency are standardised. Construction of the Great Wall begins.

206 BC– AD 220 Han Dynasty. Trade routes developed along the Silk Road to Central Asia and the Middle East. Paper invented. Astronomers learn to predict eclipses. Buddhism arrives from India.

220–65 The Three Kingdoms. Internecine warfare between the states of Shu, Wei and Wu.

581–618 Sui Dynasty. Peace and unity are restored and a new capital is established at Luoyang. Work on the Grand Canal commences.

618–907 Tang Dynasty. A golden age for music, art and poetry, science and economic growth. The capital at Chang'an becomes one of the world's great cities. Chinese porcelain acquires a reputation for excellence.

A ceramic from the Tang Dynasty displayed at the Shanghai Museum

Gunpowder invented. Woodblock printing begun and printing presses established. Empress Wu, China's first woman ruler, poisons her way to power and rules (690–705).

907–60 The Five Dynasties and Ten Kingdoms. A period of further internecine warfare.

907–1125 Liao Dynasty. Established by Khitan Tartars from Mongolia. Beijing's first turn at being a capital city, albeit one that controlled only northern China.

960–1279 Song Dynasty. Capital at Kaifeng, in the northern province of Henan, but later transferred to Hangzhou, dividing the dynasty into northern and Southern Song periods. Opera developed, literature and landscape painting begin to flourish. Tea becomes popular throughout China.

1279–1368 Yuan Dynasty. The Mongols invade China and Kublai Khan sets up his capital at Dadu, present-day Beijing. Marco Polo visits China during this period.

1368–1644 Ming Dynasty. Han Chinese overthrow the Yuan and re-establish Chinese rule over a unified China. Zijin Cheng (the Forbidden City) is built at Beijing, the first time Beijing becomes the national capital of a truly Chinese dynasty. Maritime explorations to Indian Ocean and East Africa.

1644–1911 Qing Dynasty. Invading Manchus from the northeast take advantage of an imperial court weakened by corruption to capture Beijing. Western colonial powers begin incursions into China.

1839–42 Chinese authorities seize Western opium at Canton, leading to the First Opium War the following year. China faces a century of imperialism.

1842 Treaty of Nanjing ends the war. Five treaty ports are opened to foreigners. Hong Kong is ceded to Britain.

1850–64 The anti-Manchu Taiping Rebellion devastates China.

1862 Dowager Empress Cixi is named regent and

becomes de facto ruler of China.

1895 Treaty of Shimonoseki brings Sino-Japanese War (1894–5) to an end. Taiwan ceded to Japan.

1900 The Boxer Rebellion, an anti-foreign uprising, disrupts Beijing and encourages further foreign intervention.

1908 Emperor Pu Yi, China's last emperor, accedes to the throne.

1911 Emperor Pu Yi and the Qing Empire are overthrown by Sun Yatsen and like-minded nationalist revolutionaries. A period of instability follows.

1912 Republic of China is established on 1 January.

1921 Chinese Communist Party is formed in Shanghai.

1931 Japan invades Manchuria.

1934 Chinese Communists, led by Mao Zedong, begin their epic Long March.

1935 The Long March ends.

1937 War breaks out between China and Japan following the Marco Polo Bridge incident.

1945 Japan is defeated and Taiwan is returned to China.

1946 Civil war between Communists and Nationalist forces (Kuomintang) resumes.

1949 Communist forces control the mainland. Nationalist forces retreat to Taiwan. Mao Zedong declares founding of the People's Republic of China in Tiananmen Square on 1 October.

1957 Mao launches the Hundred Flowers Movement. By the end of the year more than 300,000 'rightists' are banished to the countryside or jailed.

1958 Mao launches the disastrous Great Leap Forward (a programme of rapid industrialisation), which leads to famine. Communes established.

1966 The Cultural Revolution begins as Mao issues a directive criticising senior

	party officials. Bands of 'Red Guards' wreak havoc across the country.
1972	US President Richard Nixon visits Beijing, ending more than two decades of official enmity following the Korean War.
1976	Premier Zhou Enlai passes away in January. Mao dies in September.
1978	Deng Xiaoping assumes power and crushes ultra-leftist factions.
1989	The government kills hundreds of student demonstrators at Tiananmen Square in Beijing.
1990	Deng installs Jiang Zemin as his successor. The first stock exchange opens in Shanghai.
1997	Deng dies. Hong Kong is returned to the mainland.
1998	The Communist Party of China celebrates its first 50 years of rule. Portugal returns Macao to the Chinese.
2000	China joins the World Trade Organization.
2003	Businessmen are encouraged to join the Chinese Communist Party.
2004	Rights of private property are restored for the first time since 1949.
2008	Southern China is hit by the worst snow storms in 50 years, paralysing large parts of Guandong Province. China hosts the Olympics in Beijing.

THE CULTURAL REVOLUTION

Unleashed in 1966, this was Mao Zedong's attempt to free the Communist Party, society and culture from the 'old' values that were preventing the attainment of 'pure' Communism. For ten years, groups of 'Red Guards' composed of young workers and students were encouraged to attack all manifestations of authority except, of course, Mao himself. Temples were desecrated, schools and universities closed, teachers and factory managers tormented or worse, and millions sent to the countryside to 'learn from the peasants'. Finally the groups turned on each other. Cooler heads realised the country was descending into anarchy and called an end to the movement. Still, an inestimable price was paid in destroyed lives and property, including by the Guards themselves, who entered adulthood ignorant of all except chanted slogans. After Mao's death, the chaos was blamed on the 'Gang of Four', four top Communist Party officials, including Mao's wife, Jiang Qing, who later died in prison.

Politics

China's current political dynasty has clearly given priority to stability and material prosperity over democracy. Deng Xiaoping once remarked that the most basic of human rights is the right to eat. Still, it can be argued that only when the people feel that their interests are truly best represented by the government can true stability and prosperity flourish in China.

The People's Republic of China was proclaimed in 1949 after the Communist forces of Mao Zedong won a hard-fought war against the Nationalist Kuomintang government of Chiang Kaishek. Chiang fled to Taiwan (then known as Formosa). China became – or more accurately continued to be – a one-party state, this time with the Chinese Communist Party in the driving seat. Under the government's first five-year plan, great stress was placed on nationalisation, the development of heavy industry and the collectivisation of agriculture, the intention being to drag China from the feudal age into the modern world. The Great Leap Forward, initiated in 1958, emphasised the development of local political structures under Communist Party control, and the establishment of rural communes. It also led to the death of millions in the famine that followed.

Intellectuals had begun to chafe under the restrictions placed on their freedom of expression. In partial response to this, the party launched its Hundred Flowers Movement under the slogan: 'Let a Hundred Flowers Bloom and a Hundred Schools of Thought Contend'. Those who took advantage of the apparent openness to voice anti-government opinions were identified and purged. The struggle continued between those who supported Mao in preaching revolutionary fervour, and the pragmatists who were willing to ditch much Communist dogma in favour of progress – with the clear understanding that the party had absolutely no intention of relaxing its monopoly on political power.

As Mao and his supporters felt their control of the party slipping away to what they considered 'capitalist roaders', Mao struck back with the Great Proletarian Cultural Revolution in 1966. For ten years, China remained in the grip of an ailing Mao's obsession with permanent revolution. Youthful

'Red Guards' launched a wave of terror in which opponents were banished to the countryside, tortured or killed. Mao's death in 1976 and the arrest of his closest supporters (the so-called Gang of Four, including Mao's wife, Jiang Qing) cleared the way for Deng Xiaoping, who became the Communist Party Chairman in 1978.

Deng introduced more pragmatic policies in the economic sphere, famously announcing 'it is glorious to be rich', and flirting openly with capitalism, releasing the native energy and business skills of the Chinese, and allowing them to benefit personally while developing the country's overall economy.

Deng's legacy, however, was permanently scarred by the events of 3 and 4 June 1989, when his government ordered the suppression of pro-democracy demonstrations in Beijing, sparking the so-called 'Tiananmen Massacre'. Many innocent civilians and protesting students were mown down by the People's Liberation Army (PLA). Estimates of the dead range from 200 to 300 (Chinese government figures) to as high as 3,000 (Chinese student associations and Chinese Red Cross figures).

Following the death of Deng in 1997 more freedom has been gradually given, although the Chinese Communist Party continues to hold ultimate power. Recent years have even seen a small-scale introduction of a voting system in some areas to elect village leaders and communities, pointing the way towards a kind of democracy. Indeed, former President Jiang Zemin and former premier Zhu Rongji did their utmost to promote international trade to make sure the open-door policy never slams shut – China's hosting of world summits such as APEC (Asia-Pacific Economic Cooperation) and of course the 2008 Olympics are major examples. China is today a member of the World Trade Organization; and Hong Kong and Macao's return to China have heralded a new tolerance of Western-style government. Despite many changes, political freedom lags far behind economic freedom. However, by and large, ordinary Chinese are focused on their new-found prosperity, while the Communist authorities concentrate on boosting international prestige and national pride through China's burgeoning space exploration programme and the 2008 Olympics, both of which are designed to show a more open and progressive face to the world.

The Chinese flag

Culture

The south is considerably more culturally diverse than the north, and is home to most of the country's ethnic minorities. Most of China's major seaports are in the south, and the region has supplied most of the world's 'overseas' Chinese, who took their culinary traditions with them; what Westerners know as Chinese food is usually from the south. Southerners are considered less conservative, more fun-loving, talkative and, by their northern brethren, a tad unscrupulous.

Largely for linguistic reasons, it is the visual arts of China which are most appealing to non-Chinese. Chinese ceramics (*see feature pp60–61*) are a wonder to behold, from delicate blue and white porcelains and deeply hued celadons to unglazed Yixing teapots. Jade and other stone (as well as the currently disfavoured ivory) carvings are created with exquisite detail. China still produces fine silks, often intricately embroidered.

The Chinese, however, consider painting and calligraphy their highest visual art form. Traditional paintings are usually watercolours painted on scrolls of either paper or silk, which in some cases tell a story which develops as the scroll is unfurled. This is aided by the regular use of calligraphy in Chinese paintings; some scrolls consist only of highly stylised Chinese characters.

Traditional Chinese music is typically instrumental, which makes it more accessible to foreigners. Classical Chinese music is both graceful and calming and an ideal accompaniment to a good cup of green tea. Typically a small ensemble is composed of string, wind and percussion instruments.

Chinese music in a much less calming genre finds a home in opera. In fact, between the lilting dialogues and clashing gongs, the opera can be quite cacophonous, but great fun. Elaborate costumes, acrobatic clown roles and fantastic masks of make-up enliven the

FACE, AND HOW NOT TO LOSE IT

Face is important in China. It shows itself in subtle ways, particularly with foreign visitors. The more irritated a foreigner becomes at the lack of reaction (inscrutability, if you will) of a Chinese who doesn't seem to be getting the message, the smaller he becomes in the eye of the beholder. This can make travelling in China hard on the nerves, because the country throws up many situations that seem to call for vociferous complaint.

The Chinese are not averse to shouting among themselves, but foreigners should always be patient and understanding.

Masked dancers at a festival in Guizhou

proceedings, especially for foreigners, who cannot be expected to follow the dialogue. Shanghai is famous for its particular style of opera, called *kunqu.*

Chinese traditional architecture is world-renowned for its distinctively elaborate yet graceful architectural forms, and Shanghai abounds with fine examples of this heritage, despite the depredations of time, wars and now development. The complex symmetrical plans, colourful pavilions and curved roofs are not only attractive, but culturally relevant, since many relate to traditional beliefs, such as the curved eaves, which function to launch malevolent forces back to the sky. *Feng shui*, or geomancy, which combines mystical formulas and design common sense, dictated classical architectural design and led to buildings of grace, style and practicality.

The modern art and cultural environment of China is also not without interest. Chinese films, such as *Red Sorghum* and *Farewell My Concubine*, have received international acclaim, even while they are officially banned in China. Chinese painters and architects have established a reputation for innovation rather than mere derivative copes of Western motifs, and Shanghai is clearly the modern art capital of China. While Shanghainese certainly enjoy window-shopping in the glitzy Western-style malls of Nanjing Road and the Bund, they can also be found taking visible delight in the traditional architecture of the city's parks and gardens.

Confucianism, Taoism and Buddhism

Confucianism

The stereotypical 'Chinaman' of Hollywood films was always ready with some anodyne saying from Confucius, reflecting the fact that Confucian thought still permeates Chinese society, as it has done for 2,500 years. Many educated Chinese can quote knowledgeably from the great philosopher, whose real name was Kong Fuzi, meaning the Master Kong. Born in the 6th century BC at Qufu in the state of Lu (present-day Shandong Province), Confucius spent most of his life as a government official. The *Confucian Analects*, compiled after his death, are a collection of his sayings and actions, which are themselves based on ancient Chinese teachings and precepts. Confucius believed the origins of nature are to be found in the yin–yang, passive–active principles, which form a harmony when combined. In practice, he stressed social justice, filial piety and the obligations of the ruler towards the ruled and vice versa. The religious element in his teaching was based on the notion that if individuals and society behaved properly, heaven would leave them in peace.

Taoism

Taoism is based on the teachings of Lao Zi, meaning the Old Master, a 6th-century BC philosopher. Nothing is known about the life of Lao Zi (who may actually be legendary). His teachings, compiled in the 3rd century BC, were at least partly in competition with those of Confucius. In the collection of sacred Taoist texts called *Dao De Jing*, the Tao, or

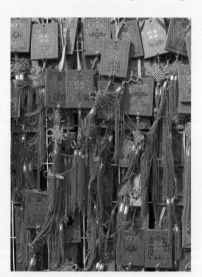

Red tassels symbolise good fortune

Way, is the hidden principle at the heart of the universe, a principle which can be touched by those prepared to live in harmony with nature and the environment. This was in contrast to the focus on right behaviour and good deeds advocated by Confucius. As Taoism developed, its belief system also incorporated the yin–yang (female–male) system of balancing opposites.

Buddhism

Buddhism arrived in China from India. Karma is Buddhism's main doctrine: the belief that good and evil deeds beget their own reward, both in this life and more so in the future through reincarnation. By the time of its widespread acceptance in China, Buddhism had undergone significant changes. The concept of Paradise became a key part of Chinese Buddhism in the Mahayana form called Chan in China, a variation of which took root in Japan as Zen. The idea that a Buddhist monk should be able to look after himself led to the foundation of the Shaolin Monastery near Dengfeng, in Henan Province, where the kung fu form of self-defence combat was developed.

Modern beliefs

Today, the officially atheist government has softened its stance

Incense is offered along with prayers at all temples

on religious practice and many sacred sites of all faiths have even been restored. The Han Chinese are not (nor ever were) adherents of a single faith, but choose elements of each religion that appeal to them to form a syncretic belief system. Muslim Chinese are an exception to this. Christianity is also gaining popularity, especially among the young. Older people continue to go on pilgrimages to temples or holy mountains, and the younger generation now make tentative and awkward, but visibly heartfelt, offerings at religious sites.

Festivals and events

Festivals form an important part of China's respect for the past, although not all are public holidays. This is a selection of the more important festivals celebrated either nationally or specifically in Shanghai or various other locations throughout southern China. Note that traditional Chinese festivals are based on the lunar calendar, so the specific date varies from year to year. If you're going to be in China around the approximate dates, ask around for specifics.

Spring Festival

Late January or early February. Also known as Chinese New Year. Mainly celebrated at home, but public parks fill up with families in their new finery, houses are decorated and firecrackers chase away the evil spirits.

Lantern Festival

Mid-February–mid-March. Home-made lanterns are displayed on the 15th day of the first lunar month, a full moon marking the end of New Year's celebrations.

Tomb Sweep Day

5 April. Honouring ancestors by cleaning their tombs and placing flowers on them.

Dai Nationality Water Sprinkling Festival

13–15 April. In the southern Yunnanese city of Jinghong, people of the Dai ethnic group celebrate life by splashing water on each other; the more water, the luckier and healthier one will be.

Longhua Temple Fair

Late April–early May. Acrobats and musicians perform in the streets around Shanghai's famous temple.

Dragon Boat Festival

June. Held on the full moon of the fifth lunar month, decorated traditional boats are raced in the honour of Qu Yuan, a poet who drowned himself in the 3rd century BC to protest imperial corruption. In Shanghai, races are held on the Huangpu River.

Yunnan Torch Festival

23–25 July. A wide-ranging cultural festival, culminating in a torchlight procession. Originally a festival of the Yi people, it is now celebrated by the Dai and Naxi minorities in Dali and Lijiang.

Sichuan Torch Festival

23–28 July. Torchlight parades and other cultural performances of minority nationalities throughout Sichuan Province.

Xuedun Festival

Variable dates, usually in August. The Tibetan yoghurt-banquet festival, held in Lhasa, includes performances of traditional Tibetan opera and dance.

Suzhou International Silk Festival

20–25 September. During this fashion show, the city's imperial gardens are illuminated and used for garden parties.

Chengdu International Panda Festival

24–28 September. Symposium on panda conservation, and visits to nearby Wolong Nature Reserve.

Mid-Autumn Festival

Late September–early October. Essentially a harvest festival, celebrated throughout the country on the full moon of the fifth lunar month. Temples are lighted in the evening, and locals have barbeques in the parks, eating moon cakes while admiring the moon.

Shanghai Formula One Race

Early October. Hardly traditional, yet this grand prix circuit race attracts aficionados of motor sport from around the world.

West Lake International Tour Boat Festival

5–7 October. On the old imperial lake at Hangzhou, a feast of traditional costumes and gaily decorated tour boats.

Three Gorges Art Festival

20–25 October (every second year). A celebration in Yichang (Hubei Province) of the arts and crafts of the Yangzi River's Three Gorges area.

Kaizhai Festival

This Islamic festival celebrates the end of the fasting month of Ramadan. Since Islam uses a strictly lunar calendar, the three-day festival can fall any time during the Gregorian calendar. Near any mosque you will find music, sweetmeats and general merry-making.

Festivals and events

Hong Kong's celebrated Dragon Boat Festival Race is a test of skill and stamina

Highlights

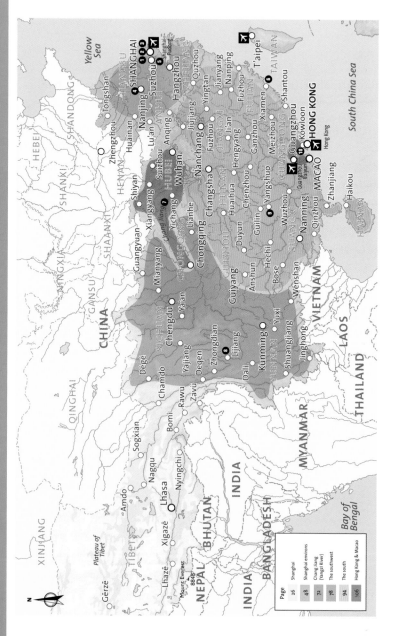

1 The Bund This promenade along the Huangpu River in central Shanghai is both a breath of fresh air and a history lesson. On one side of the river the neo-classical architecture of the 1930s exemplifies the era when foreigners ruled the roost, but across the river in Pudong, the futuristic skyline represents China's current aspirations.

2 Nanshi Shanghai's Old Town has been sanitised for the tourist trade, but getting off the main streets is a trip back in time.

3 The Former French Concession Start in Fuxing Park and head west towards Huaihai District and you'll see the luxurious villas where the French, as well as well-connected Chinese, lived and enjoyed the good life in the early 20th century.

4 Nanjing Historically significant and attractive, with tree-lined avenues, lakes and gardens, this walled city is situated on the banks of the Yangzi. The nearby Purple Mountain overlooks the city.

5 Suzhou Only a short drive from Shanghai but a world apart, this is the best place to observe classical Chinese gardens, and some of the city's fabled canals still flow.

6 Xiamen Known in the West as Amoy, this island city just off the coast of Fujian Province has offered a bustling seaport atmosphere and colonial architecture since it was first occupied by the Portuguese in the 17th century.

7 Yangzi River cruise So far, the Three Gorges Dam seems to have changed little of the magnificent gorges; in fact, the rising waters have allowed boats to cruise the previously unnavigable tributaries of China's longest river.

8 Lijiang This small town located in the northwest of Yunnan is a UNESCO World Heritage Site. Melting snow from the Jade Dragon Mountain and a spring feed the canals that criss-cross the town, accented here and there by quaint old stone bridges.

9 Yangshuo A visit to Yangshuo, with its incredible karst mountains, beautiful rivers and emerald green rice paddies, is like stepping into a Chinese landscape painting. It is best appreciated by coupling it with a cruise to Guilin on the nearby Li River.

10 Hong Kong Although it now belongs to the People's Republic, the atmosphere here is palpably different from the rest of the country. A stunningly beautiful bay at the mouth of the Pearl River, with the best shopping in Asia.

Suggested itineraries

These itineraries will let you see as much of the destination as time allows. They are admittedly fast-paced, and individual travellers will of course have special interests and choose to focus more on some areas or types of sights longer than, or to the exclusion of, others.

Long weekend

On your first night splurge on dinner in one of the upmarket restaurants on the Bund. If you're young and restless, visit one of the clubs on Maoming Road in the former French Concession. If not, just stroll the Bund, or walk along Nanjing Road to People's Park. The next day, visit the Yu Garden, take tea at the Huxinting Teahouse, then dive into the nearby Yu Yuan Bazaar.

If you want to experience bargain hunting as the locals do it, take a cab to the Xipu Market in Zhabei District, the city's mecca for knock-offs. Bargain hard and watch your wallet. Have dinner in a French Concession villa restaurant. On your final day, slip in a bit of culture at the Shanghai Museum in People's Park, the best in the country and worthy of slow savouring. If you're adamantly opposed to museums, take a day trip to one of the water towns outside the city.

One week

Start with Shanghai, as shown for the long weekend above. Add a visit to Suzhou, which is a short drive (or train) away and can be reached in just

Cruise boat on the Huangpu River in Shanghai

Victoria Harbour from the Peak in Hong Kong

over an hour. Explore the town's renowned gardens and extensive network of canals. Ming Dynasty silk merchants thrived here and built some of China's loveliest ornamental gardens. There is no airport in Suzhou, but you will enjoy the two-hour train ride to Nanjing, which passes through beautiful rural areas and small towns. In Nanjing, visit the splendid Zhonghua Gate and the adjacent Xuanwu Lake. Climb the Purple Mountain to the Mausoleum of Dr Sun Yatsen, the 'Father of Modern China'. From Nanjing take the early morning flight to Chongqing and board a Yangzi cruise ship. Pass by striking temples high up on the river's banks and then marvel at the sheer magnitude of the Three Gorges. If time permits, a side trip on the Daning River to the Lesser Gorges is well worthwhile. Finish the cruise at China's modern pride and joy, the newly constructed Three Gorges

Dam, from where you can make your way to nearby Yichang rather than continuing to Wuhan. From Yichang take a flight to Hong Kong, where your last day can be spent decompressing in this former British colony. Take the ferry from Kowloon to Hong Kong Island and do any last-minute shopping or take the tram up to Victoria Peak and admire the stunning views of the famous harbour. In the evening, head for the waterfront promenade on the Kowloon side and watch the nightly light show that is Hong Kong Island.

Two weeks
The first week can be spent as shown above, but take an extra day to relax in Shanghai, or take the Yangzi river cruise as far as Wuhan and discover the lovely Buddhist Guiyuan Temple and its 500 *arhat* statues. The second week can start with a flight to Kunming. Explore this most temperate of Chinese towns

on foot. Don't miss the excellent museum and, if you have time, the Golden Temple north of the city. Have dinner in one of the many restaurants in and around the beautiful Green Lake Park. Then take a taxi to the outskirts of Kunming city and visit the Western Hills with their large temple complexes and outstanding views of Dianchi Lake. Fly to Lijiang in the evening. Explore the ancient city of Lijiang with its twisting cobblestone lanes and vaulted stone footbridges. Walk to the nearby Black Dragon Pool and marvel at the

One of the twin pagodas, Shuang Ta in Suzhou

towering Jade Dragon Snow Mountain. Have dinner on the main square of Si Fang Jie. From there, you can fly to Guilin via Kunming. Visit the famous Reed Flute Temple and Elephant Trunk Park. Overnight in Guilin, and then take an early morning cruise along the Li River to Yangshuo and enjoy the limestone peaks that guard the entire length of the river. Explore the charming town of Yangshuo and either cruise back upriver to Guilin or take the bus: there's no airport in Yangshuo. You can fly to Xiamen from Guilin in the morning and explore this laid-back seaport. In the afternoon take the ten-minute ferry ride to the island of Gulang Yu and stroll the crooked lanes snaking their way around this most European of places. Your final day can be spent taking the hydrofoil from Xiamen to Hong Kong and enjoying the magnificent entry into Victoria Harbour surrounded by the gleaming towers of modern finance.

Longer visits

Continue north from Lijiang to Tiger Leaping Gorge and see the Yangzi River thundering through the gorge, then on to Shangri-La with its Tibetan pagodas and snow-capped mountains. From Deqen it's a five-day drive in a 4-WD vehicle to Lhasa or a two-hour flight from the Shangri-La airport in Zhongdian. However you choose to reach Tibet, take time to acclimatise to the altitude.

Canal in Suzhou

Shanghai

The largest city in China, with 19 million inhabitants, Shanghai is big, bustling, stylish, commercial, optimistic and sure of itself. The politicos in Beijing may make the rules, but Shanghai's business-minded citizens are making the money and setting the trends. The constantly changing skyline of Pudong New Area now rivals that of Hong Kong as China's image of prosperity, with buildings such as the Pearl Oriental TV Tower and the Grand Hyatt (Jin Mao Tower), the highest hotel and bar in the world.

Pudong radiates a feeling of space-age technology, in complete contrast to the conservative formality of the Bund directly opposite. The old Chinese district of Nanshi, and Huaihai, the former French Concession, show other facets of this fascinating metropolis.

Shanghai began life as a fishing village, and later as a port receiving goods carried down the Yangzi River. From 1842 onwards, in the aftermath of the first Opium War, the British opened a 'concession' in Shanghai where drug dealers and other traders could operate undisturbed. French, Italians, Germans, Americans and Japanese all followed. By the 1920s and 1930s, Shanghai was a boom town and an international byword for dissipation. When the Communists won power in 1949, they transformed Shanghai into a model of the Revolution.

It is hard for infrastructure projects, however big, to keep pace with the city's growth. The recently completed ring road has already become a traffic-

jammed nightmare for motorists, and the ever-expanding subway system becomes overloaded almost as fast as new sections open.

Huaihai: the former French Concession

Lying directly to the west of Luwan and covering roughly the area between Fuxing Park and Huaihai Road, this area is rich in elegant French colonial architecture, relaxing parks, sights of historical interest and some of Shanghai's best nightlife.

The Shanghai Art Museum at night

Shanghai

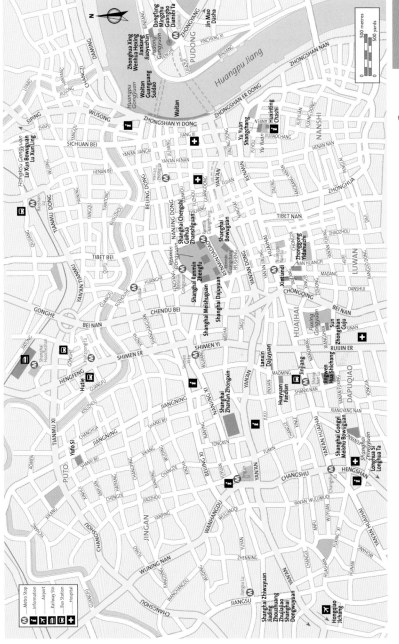

Shanghai

Fuxing Gongyuan (Fuxing Park)

Built by the French and opened in 1909, this large and leafy expanse still serves its original purpose as respite from the city's noise and odours. Old men play chess, lovers canoodle on benches, and kids frolic (there is a small amusement park within the grounds), all under the benevolent gaze of Karl Marx and Frederick Engels, the founders of Communism, represented by bronze statues. The park is also a popular venue for outdoor concerts.
Chongqing. Open: 6am–6pm. Admission charge. Metro: Shanxi Nan Lu or Huangpi Nan Lu.

Jin Mao Tower in Pudong

Maoming Lu (Maoming Road)

This road runs through the heart of the French Concession and has something for everyone. Starting at the north end, at the intersection with Changle, is the **Lyceum Theatre (Lanxin Dajuyuan)**, built in the 1930s as home to the British Shanghai Amateur Dramatic Society, and the place where the famous ballerina Margot Fonteyn performed as a child. It now hosts acrobatic performances and Chinese opera. Across the street is the **Okura Garden Hotel (Huayuan Fandian)**, which began life as the Cercle Sportif Français and later was Mao's private residence in Shanghai. The 20 tennis courts of the French era have been reduced, but the grounds, architecture and interiors are superb.

Continuing south on Maoming Road, you enter Shanghai's wildest bar district, at least in the evenings. It's not rough or raunchy (that distinction belongs to Julu Road in Jingan) but the largely local crowd is certainly ready to party. In the day there are some interesting boutiques in the area.

Maoming Road ends at the **Jingwen Flower Market (Jingwen Hua Shichang)**, where elaborate and beautifully presented cut flower arrangements are displayed, most likely soon to be used at the equally elaborate wedding receptions that are *de rigueur* for young couples in Shanghai.
Metro: Shanxi Nan Lu.

Shanghai

Sun Yatsen's Residence

Republic and Taiwan. Sun lived in this unimpressive villa (by the standards of the neighbourhood) with his wife, whose sister met her future husband Chiang Kaishek here. It is still furnished in 1920s style, and displays various mementoes of Dr Sun, including photographs and his medical case.
Xiangshan, near Fuxing Park.
Tel: (021) 6437 2954. Open: Mon–Sat 9am–4.30pm. Closed: Sun. Admission charge. Metro: Shanxi Nan Lu or Huangpi Nan Lu.

Shanghai Gongyi Meishu Bowuguan (Shanghai Museum of Arts and Crafts)

Designed by the famous Hungarian architect Ladislau Hudec, who created many art deco masterpieces in 1930s Shanghai, this museum bears passing similarity to a smaller version of the White House in Washington. It now houses an arts and crafts research institute where visitors can observe creative activities such as embroidery, kite manufacture, carving in various materials and painting. Many of the goods produced are for sale, and there is an antique shop in the basement.
79 Fenyang. Tel: (021) 6437 0509. Open: 9am–5pm. Admission charge.
Metro: Changshu Lu.

Sun Zhongshan Guju (Sun Yatsen's Residence)

The 'Father of Modern China' lived here from 1920 to 1924, in a house bought for him by Chinese Canadians. Sun is unique in being revered by the governments of both the People's

Xintiandi

This new construction of traditional Shanghai architecture is filled with trendy but, in contrast to Maoming Road, squeaky clean bars and restaurants. Starbucks and McDonald's also have a foot in the door here. The name means 'new heaven and earth', which is quite appropriate since it's the favourite haven of Shanghai's *nouveaux riches*. It's a great place for al fresco dining in the evening. One has to appreciate the irony that it lies adjacent to the Museum of the First National Congress of the Chinese Communist Party (*see p32*). There are some interesting shops, a boutique hotel, a micro brewery, a post office specialising in commemorative issues, and a museum detailing Shanghai's architectural heritage. All this is packed into a relatively small and well-maintained two-block area.
Intersection of Taicang and Madang. Open: morning–late. Metro: Huangpi Nan Lu.

Chinese gardens

Outside the walls of a Chinese garden may be some of the noisiest and most polluted streets on earth. Inside, the peace that reigns has inspired poets and painters over centuries, and still has the power to help visitors unwind from a stressful day, while breathing the scented air of tranquillity. Gardens are one of the most precious legacies of China's 5,000-year-old civilisation, and they continue to delight the senses. A Chinese garden is much more than nature in miniature; it represents the essence of nature.

The first recorded Chinese botanical garden was established at Chang'an (Xian) in 111 BC, although China's devotion to flowers, as indicated by poetry and painting, reaches back thousands of years earlier. A common name for China is 'the Flowery Land'. Yet flowers are not the principal element in a Chinese garden. Pools, goldfish, trees, rocks and white walls (symbolising mist) provide more than a setting for floral displays. They bring the vastness and changeability of the natural world down to a human scale, creating a place that is truly fit for meditation.

The natural world reduced to human scale: ancient gardens in Shanghai…

...and Suzhou

Change is characteristic of nature, so observing change is an integral part of the inspiration and design of a garden. Pavilions are laid out so that different aspects of the garden can be observed as the seasons unfold. Peonies are the stars of spring; pools laden with water-lilies the highlight of summer; in autumn, chrysanthemums and orchids take centre stage; and the stark effects of bare rock and chill winds add inspiration to winter afternoons in heated pavilions. Wide vistas alternate with constricted views, adding to the contrasting effects that are being sought.

China's most famous gardens are to be found in Suzhou, west of Shanghai. The town's mild climate played an important role in the formation of these gardens. At one time the town boasted more than 280 private gardens and today there are almost 70 still in good condition. The great gardens of Suzhou are mainly from the Ming and Qing periods.

Chinese gardens are not limited to China. The New York Chinese Scholar's Garden on Staten Island was constructed by Chinese artisans from Suzhou as recently as 1998. Vancouver's Dr Sun Yat-Sen Classical Chinese Garden, completed in 1985, was the first classical, Suzhou-style garden outside of China.

Zhonggong Yidahuizhi (Museum of the First National Congress of the Communist Party of China)

This is the house where the Communist Party of China was inaugurated in a clandestine meeting within the French Concession area in July 1921, with Mao Zedong one of the 13 delegates. It is a surprisingly bourgeois setting for such an event, an attractive *shikumen* (stone gate) house. A table set with 13 chairs and teacups commemorates the meeting, but the sad truth is that 11 of the 13 were killed in later purges or defected to the Kuomintang. An interesting exhibition hall adjoins the house.

76 Xingye. Tel: (021) 5383 2171. Open: 9am–5pm. Admission charge, but admission free after 4pm. Metro: Huangpi Nan Lu.

Nanshi (Old Town)

The name means 'southern city' and it is appropriately located south of the major thoroughfare of Yan'an Road, bordering the Huangpu River, aeons away from the prestigious Bund. Now sometimes called the 'Old City', it is the part of Shanghai where all the Chinese were supposed to live during the concession era. It is now the most traditional part of Shanghai, with winding alleys and atmospheric shops. The Fangbang Yan'an area, Yu Yuan (Yu Gardens) and Shangchang (Bazaar) have all been restored and are on the tourist maps, but venture away from this section of Nanshi and you'll see a truly different side of Shanghai.

Fangbang Zhong Lu (Fangbang Yan'an Area)

Fangbang Central Road is the heart of Shanghai's reinvented Old Town. The west end is entered through a traditional gateway and is called 'Old Shanghai Street'. It's a street filled with shops selling reproduction antiques and all varieties of *chinoiserie*. The quality

The Gateway to the Old Town and Yu Yuan Bazaar area

and prices of goods are favourable compared to those in other Shanghai tourist venues, although bargaining is a must. It's all a bit of a show, with the municipality sponsoring 'impromptu' musical performances, but it's good fun.

Huxinting Chashi (Mid-Lake Pavilion Teahouse)

Located between the Yu Gardens and the Yu Yuan Bazaar (*see listings below*), this was once the home of the mandarin who built the gardens, but became a public teahouse in 1855. Climb to the second floor and enjoy a relaxing pot of Chinese tea overlooking the gardens and crowds below. As the name suggests, the teahouse is approached across an artificial lake by a stone causeway of rectangular zigzags called the 'Bridge of Nine Turnings' designed not to impede human visitors, but rather evil spirits and malicious ghosts who, of course, can only travel in straight lines.

Next to the Yu Yuan Bazaar and Yu Gardens. Open: 8.30am–10pm. Tel: (021) 6373 6950. Bus: 6, 11, 66, 930.

Yu Yuan (Yu Gardens)

Adjacent to the Yu Yuan Bazaar, but not part of it, are the famous Yu Gardens, the best example of a traditional Suzhou garden to be found in Shanghai. The Chinese character 'yu' means 'comfortable ease', but on weekends and holidays the crowds here make this a scarce commodity. A Ming-

Traditional buildings in Yu Yuan Bazaar area

Dynasty mandarin built these gardens over a period of 20 years, beginning in 1559. Only 2 hectares (5 acres) in size, they include 30 pavilions organised into six distinct sections. In the classical scheme of Chinese gardens, they are intended to create a world in microcosm, with rocks recreating mountains and caves, and strategically planted trees and shrubs representing forests. The sections are divided by vaulted bridges and meandering causeways.

218 Anren. Tel: (021) 6328 3251. Open: 8.30am–5pm. Admission charge. Bus: 6, 11, 66, 930.

Chinese opera and circus

Chinese opera

Chinese drama, including what is known abroad as Beijing opera, began rather late in China's cultural evolution, during the Yuan Dynasty (1279–1368), although it drew on older storytelling traditions. Beijing opera (which is only one of 300 different forms of traditional opera) only really flowered during the Qing Dynasty, from the 18th century. It is characterised by exaggerated and stylised actions (generally performed by men), and high-pitched singing accompanied by a piercing string and percussion ensemble. The Shanghai version, called *kunqu*, uses woodwind instruments rather than string instruments. It is not to everyone's taste, although it is interesting to see at least once. The themes are usually romantic in the broad sense, with characters using their skill to overcome natural disasters, rebellion or some other calamity. The high-pitched singing and music styles developed out of the need to project over chattering crowds in

Chinese opera is a highly stylised art

Chinese circus artists' skills are world famous

such noisy performance venues as markets and teahouses. Authentic Chinese opera is still a form of street theatre, but you can also see it in the more formal context of the theatre. Visually, the costumes are the most striking feature, and the style of the clothes and of the make-up gives clues to the characters' true natures.

Circus

Chinese circus does not involve animals and is all about acrobatics, performed by troupes and individuals whose skills are legendary. Plate-spinning and performing handstands on a pagoda of chairs are the least of the marvels. The skills originated with popular street theatre and are emblematic of religious festivals, sacrificial rites, and themes from daily life, although they have since moved to the more sophisticated venue of the gymnasium.

Acrobatics have a long history in China, with the first records dating back more than 2,000 years to the time of Qin Shi Huang, the First Emperor. As in Europe, families developed particular skills and formed troupes, performing a variety of different acts. By 1949, the acrobatic arts had fallen into decline due to constant warring across the country. Fortunately, the new Communist authorities realised that this art form was of and from the people and made great efforts to preserve the skills. Consequently, in 1950 the first state acrobatic troupe was formed in Beijing. Today, there are more than 250 Chinese troupes touring China and the world.

Pudong skyline from Suzhou Creek

Yu Yuan Shangchang (Yu Yuan Bazaar)
Less focused on the foreign tourist
market than Fangbang Road, this
favourite shopping venue of locals was
recently created in Ming-Dynasty style.
The atmosphere is quite intense, with a
pulsating mass of humanity apparently
intent on shopping until it drops.
Named for the celebrated Yu Gardens
right next door, this conglomeration of
shops and an indoor mall sells a wide
range of traditional Chinese arts and
crafts.
Halfway along Fangbang Zhong,
just to the east of Jiujiaochang.
Open: 9am–9pm. Tel: (021) 6328 3251.
Bus: 6, 11, 66, 930.

Pudong

Until 1990, this part of Shanghai
(the name means 'east of the

Huangpu River') was a mixture of
agricultural land and slums, and so
insignificant that no one bothered to
build a bridge to it from Shanghai
proper. Now it is home to the most
luxurious hotels in Shanghai, the
fanciest office towers, and the Stock
Exchange.

Dongfang Mingzhu Guangbo Dianshi Ta (The Oriental Pearl Tower)

Opened in 1995 and consisting of
11 spheres (the pearls) of various
sizes connected by three columns, this
468-m (1,535-ft) tower is the icon
of futuristic Shanghai. The locals are
quite proud of the structure, but
visitors are sometimes left wondering
why. It is undeniably impressive, and
most attractive if viewed from across
the river when it is illuminated at

night. The tower is open to the public and has three observation levels, all of which offer superb views on a clear day. The highest rests at 350m (1,148ft) above ground, and there is a revolving restaurant part of the way up.
South end of Pudong Gongyuan, Lujiazui. Tel: (021) 5879 1888. Open: 8am–10pm. Admission charge. Metro: Lujiazui.

Zhonghua Xing Wenhua Hexing Jiankang Jiaoyuzhan (China Sex Culture Exhibition)

The aim is to inform rather than titillate, and it largely succeeds, since few Westerners find foot binding or the castration of eunuchs to be in line with their ideas of eroticism. It is surprisingly tasteful, and features interesting paintings and ceramics from earlier periods of Chinese history. To set the mood for something a bit odd, travel here via the Bund Sightseeing Tunnel from the Bund.
2789 Binjiang. Tel (021) 5888 6000. Open: 8am–10pm. Admission charge. Metro: Lujiazui.

Renmin Guangchang (People's Square)

This is the geographic centre of metropolitan Shanghai and underneath it the various lines of the Shanghai Metro converge into a giant interchange. Above ground it is in many ways the city's cultural and recreational heart. During the concession era, the area was the elegant Shanghai Race Course, where

The Oriental Pearl TV Tower, Zhongyin Building and BOCOM Financial Tower in Pudong

millionaires raced their fine thoroughbreds.

Renmin Gongyuan (People's Park), at the north end, is home to the neo-classical Shanghai Art Museum. In the central paved area, where Mao once greeted throngs of Red Guards, you will now find the Shanghai Grand Theatre, as well as **Shanghai Renmin Zhengfu (Shanghai City Hall)** and **Shanghai Chengshi Guihua Zhanshiguan (Shanghai Urban Planning Museum)**. In the verdant southern end lies the superb Shanghai Museum (*see listing below*). Aside from these notable attractions, the area is a welcome green lung in the heart of the city or, in the paved and open centre, Shanghai's best venue for kite flying.
Metro: Renmin Guangchang.

Shanghai Bowuguan (Shanghai Museum)

At the south end of People's Square, this is truly the jewel of the area, partly for the intrinsic elegance of its design, but mainly for its excellent contents and state-of-the-art displays. This is a real treasure-trove of Chinese art, culture and history, holding more than 120,000 artefacts representing almost five millennia of continuous civilisation. It takes a full day to appreciate the cultural treasures on display here.

The museum was designed by a local architect to represent a *ding*, or ancient three-legged bronze ceremonial vessel. It was completed in 1996. The museum

houses ten permanent galleries displayed over four floors, as well as three temporary exhibition halls. There is also a museum shop selling high-quality replicas of some of the most famous pieces on display.

Every aspect of Chinese visual art is displayed here, from bronzeware to ceramics, paintings, calligraphy, jade carving and furniture, each in their own distinctive galleries, organised by historical period. The pieces are well captioned in English, but the excellent

Plaza 66 building looms over the People's Park area of Shanghai

audio tours are highly recommended.
Southern end of People's Square.
Tel: (021) 6372 3500. Open: Mon–Fri
9am–5pm, Sat 9am–8pm. Closed: Sun.
Admission charge. Metro: Renmin
Guangchang.

Shanghai Dajuyuan (Shanghai Grand Theatre)

Designed by French architect Jean-
Marie Charpentier, a sweeping,
upwardly curved, futuristically Chinese
roof characterises this massive, ten-
storey, 1,800-seat theatre, which is
currently home to both the Shanghai
Ballet and the Shanghai Broadcast
Symphony Orchestra. Performances are
frequent, but even if you can't make
one, the interior is worth a look.
West end of People's Square. Tel: (021)
6387 5480. Open for guided tours:
9am–4.30pm. Admission charge.
Metro: Renmin Guangchang.

Shanghai Meishuguan (Shanghai Art Museum)

The interest here lies in the venue as
much as the displays; it is the former
Jockey Club of the race course, built in
1933. The clock tower, known as 'Big
Bertie', still chimes, and art deco
chandeliers illuminate the interior. The
exhibits focus on modern art and are
good, but real aficionados of the genre
will prefer the private galleries on
Moganshan Road.
325 Nanjing Xi. Tel: (021) 6372 2885.
Open: 9am–5pm. Admission charge.
Metro: Renmin Guangchang.

12th-century gold-painted Bodhisattva in
Shanghai Museum

Waitan (the Bund)

The Bund extends from **Huangpu
Gongyuan (Huangpu Park)**, along the
riverside to Yan'an. The Hindi word for
'embankment' was given by the British
to this walkway beside the Huangpu
River, bordered by 1920s and 1930s
commercial buildings. Today, the Bund,
a kind of elegant boardwalk, is a stylish
place for Shanghainese to take the
'strongly scented' air of the river (which
is certainly fresher than that of the

badly polluted city). Huangpu Park at the northern end of the Bund, formerly the British-built Municipal Gardens, is where the supposed sign 'No Dogs and Chinese Allowed' was displayed in former times. Fortunately, the Chinese are not vengeful about this, and the park is also open to foreigners (5am–10pm).

Across the river is the tall, needle-pointed mast of the Television Tower, and the recently built 88-storey Jin Mao Building that dominates the vibrant Pudong New Area.

In the other direction is the long row of solid-looking, 1920s- and 1930s-vintage buildings, with the Bank of China at No 22, and the red-fringed Shanghai Pudong Development Bank at No 12 being among the most notable.

East Nanjing Road

A stroll along the Bund is a pleasure at any time of day. In the early morning tai chi enthusiasts are out in force, and on foggy mornings the ships' sirens on the Huangpu bleat through the mist. In late afternoons, as the sun sinks behind Puxi (the major part of Shanghai, meaning 'west of the Huangpu'), it reflects off the glass towers of Pudong illuminating the traditional stone and mortar edifices along the Bund. After dark, the neo-classical buildings along the Bund are lit up, as are the futuristic towers of Pudong, creating a memorable study in contrasts.

Aside from the fresh air and atmosphere, the main attraction of the Bund is the architecture. In the 1920s, the *taipans*, as the wealthy foreign merchants were known, flush with opium profits, decided to enter more respectable trades and set up impressive offices for their new banks, insurance and shipping companies along the Bund, as well as luxurious hotels. Today they are the offices of government bureaux, international banks and, increasingly, the top floors are home to Shanghai's most exclusive restaurants.

From the base of Yan'an Road, it is possible to take a ferry across the Huangpu to Pudong, or a bit further north, where East Beijing Road meets the Bund, the **Bund Sightseeing Tunnel** also crosses the Huangpu. Be forewarned; the best that can be said about this attraction is that it is so bad that it's good. The only sightseeing is the garish displays visible through the

Hong Kong and Shanghai Banking building and the Customs House on the Bund

windows of the carriages, which are enhanced by psychedelic lighting and loud music.

Nanjing Dong Lu (East Nanjing Road)
From roughly the mid-point of the Bund, the city's – and perhaps all China's – busiest, most stylish and most expensive shopping street runs west for 1.5km (1 mile) from the Bund to People's Park. Although it is a pedestrianised street, be careful of the electric (thus silent) tourist trams and miniature trains for the kids that ply the area. Hundreds of shops and department stores do business on the street itself, along with restaurants, hotels and cafés, and there are many more of all these on the adjacent side streets. From the Bund to Central Henan Road, imaginative boutiques and street artists selling their works abound. Further west is the domain of the large department stores. You won't

find any bargains on Western branded goods in these big stores; although made in China, they're verifiably cheaper at home than here.

The interest for the visitor here is people-watching. From stylish yuppies to fluorescent-haired teenagers, families amusing their kids, and the occasional country bumpkin agog at this modern splendour, all of today's Chinese find their way to this self-proclaimed 'China's Number One Shopping Street'. Add this to a backdrop of huge electrified billboards and accompanying soundtracks, and it's more carnival than high street. Park yourself on one of the benches or at a pavement café and watch the show. When this becomes too much, head south one block and enjoy the neo-classical and art deco architecture on the old banking street of Jiujiang Road. Two blocks further south is Fuzhou Road, which is lined with bookshops.

Walk: The Bund and Nanjing Road

This walk covers the old colonial-era heart of Shanghai, which stretches along the Huangpu River to form one of the world's most stylish riverside walkways, now the focal point of an increasingly affluent Shanghai.

Allow three hours.

1 Shanghai Dasha (Shanghai Mansions)

An art deco façade graces this elegant hotel built in 1935.
Cross Waibaidu Bridge over the Suzhou creek to Huangpu Park.

2 Huangpu Gongyuan (Huangpu Park)

This pretty little riverside park once 'boasted' a notorious sign denying access to dogs and Chinese (*see p40*).
Climb the steps up to the Bund. River tour boats leave from a wharf nearby.

3 Waitan (The Bund)

The colourful, swirling mass of people, strolling along the Huangpu River, is one of China's most appealing sights (*also see pp39–41*).
At the end of the Bund, turn right into Zhongshan Yi Dong.

4 Zhongshan Yi Dong

This gives an opportunity for closer inspection of the old commercial buildings facing the river, although the overall view is better from the Bund.
Turn left at Heping Fandian (Peace Hotel) into Nanjing Dong.

5 Heping Fandian (Peace Hotel)

The Peace Hotel, formerly the Cathay Hotel, was one of the symbols of decadent old Shanghai, and still tries to retain at least a flavour of the raffish air that surrounded it. At the time of writing, the Peace Hotel was closed for renovation.
Continue on Nanjing Dong.

6 Nanjing Dong Lu (East Nanjing Road)

Nanjing Dong Lu is one of the symbols of modern Shanghai. There is a frenetic air as shoppers move along the pavement and into the well-stocked shops and department stores. Anything that would be available in a Western shopping mecca is available here.

Turn left at Shanghai Shi Diyi Baihuo Shangdian (Department Store) into Xizang Zhong.

7 Renmin Gongyuan (People's Park)

People's Park's ponds and grassy spaces are popular with the Shanghainese, who can be seen doing their pre-work tai chi exercises here in the early morning.

Continue on Xizang Zhong and turn right into Renmin Square.

8 Renmin Guangchang (People's Square)

Typical of the new urban landscape, this vast and soulless expanse of concrete, People's Square at least provides space to stretch one's legs and breathe air not directly polluted by fuming exhaust pipes. The sparklingly modern Shanghai Museum stands on its southern axis.

To return to the Shanghai Mansions area walk to Yan'an Road to wave a taxi down.

Walk: The Bund and Nanjing Road

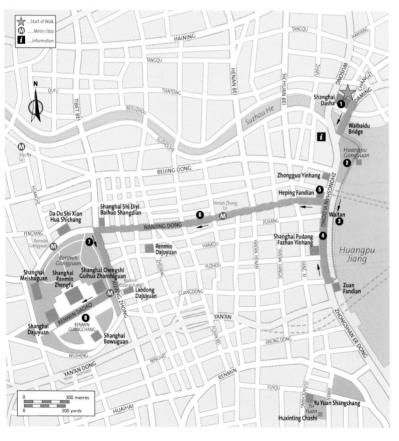

HUANGPU RIVER TRIP

The Huangpu River is a fascinating sight. The name means 'yellow creek', as it carries the silt of the Yangzi to the sea. Merchant ships, barges, ferry boats, cruise boats, junks and private craft abound, along with an occasional warship of the Chinese navy forcing its way into the waterway, in an always-changing panorama.

Shanghai can also be viewed from the river, as well as from the huge and fast-developing Pudong New Area on the east bank. Cruise boats leave from the dock on the Bund near Huangpu Park (*Tel: (021) 6374 4461*) for a one-hour cruise of Huangpu and a three- to four-hour round trip to the junction with the Yangzi River.

Outlying districts (Hongqiao, Gubei, Hongkou)

The residential areas of Hongqiao and Gubei stretch to the west of central Shanghai and offer some pleasant excursions. Hongkou, to the north, is less attractive but does offer some interesting historical diversions.

Hongkou Gongyuan (Hongkou Park)

A fair trek out along Sichuan Bei Road from the city centre leads eventually to this park, Shanghai's biggest, and a good place to observe people doing tai chi exercises in the morning. The park has an elongated lake at its heart, with islets, bridges, gardens and pavilions. On its northern shore is a waterfall. In addition, there are two important monuments to the noted Chinese writer Lu Xun (*see p45*).
Jiangwan, northern suburbs.
Open: 8am–7pm. Admission charge.
Bus: 48 from People's Square.

Longhua Si and Longhua Ta (Longhua Temple and Pagoda)

Shanghai's largest Buddhist temple is considered the finest ancient

Hundreds of gold Bodhisattva images in Longhua Temple

An avalokiteshvara image in Longhua Temple

imperial dynastic past to a modern, democratic future. The museum is only moderately interesting to non-specialists. The calligraphic inscription identifying Lu Xun's tomb was designed by Chairman Mao Zedong. A livelier atmosphere in the area prevails at the Duolun Lu Wenhua Jie (Duolun Road Cultural Street), a pedestrianised street with restored *shikumen* (stone gate) houses, bronze statues of the literati who once made this district of Shanghai their home, and interesting art galleries and cafés.

Hongkou Gongyuan. Tel: (021) 6540 2288. Museum open: 9am–3.30pm. Closed: Mon. Tomb open: 8am–7pm. Admission charge. Metro: Hongkou Zuqiuchang.

Shanghai Dongwuyuan (Shanghai Zoo)

Unlike most zoos in China, Shanghai's is not necessarily a depressing experience, because the 280 different species of animals have more space to roam.

Hongqiao, western suburbs, near Shanghai Airport. Tel: (021) 6268 7775. Open: 7am–5pm. Closed: Tue. Admission charge. Bus: 328, 911.

Shanghai Zhiwuyuan (Shanghai Botanical Gardens)

This has a fine collection of around 9,000 potted flowers and trees, and specialises in the miniature representations of nature that are the hallmarks of a Chinese garden.

monument in Shanghai. It dates from AD 247 and was built by the Emperor Sun Quan in honour of his mother. The 60-m (197-ft), seven-storey tower was rebuilt in 977. Longhua Temple has pavilions, a bell tower and a drum tower. The temple fair held here in April is famous throughout China.

Longhua, southern suburbs. Tel: (021) 6456 6085. Open: 7am–4pm. Admission charge. Metro: Shanghai Tiyuchang and then local taxi.

Lu Xun Bowuguan and Lu Xun Ling (Lu Xun Museum and Lu Xun Tomb)

Lu Xun (1881–1936) was a writer who employed his literary skills in the effort to transform China from its

The Great Hall of the Jade Buddha Temple

Longhua, southern suburbs.
Tel: (021) 6451 3369.
Open: 8am–5.30pm. Closed: Sun.
Admission charge. Metro: Shilong Lu.

Yufo Si (Jade Buddha Temple)

Built in 1882, on the southern edge of
the city, the temple was moved, lock,
stock and jade Buddha statues, to its
present location in 1918. Despite its
relatively recent provenance, the
temple complex has all the atmosphere
of more ancient places, with followers
of the Buddha praying before his
statue, wreathed in incense smoke.
The Jade Buddha on the second floor
of the main pavilion is 1.9m (6ft)
high. Carved from a single piece of
white jade, it was transported to
China from Burma in 1882. A recently
established Buddhist academy at the
temple, which has a second white

jade Buddha statue, is a sign of
the relative tolerance with which
the government now views religious
practices.
Anyuan, Puto District in the northwest.
Open: 8.30am–4.30pm. Admission
charge. Metro: Shanghai Huochezan.
Bus: 19, 76, 506.

The water towns

Like all big cities, Shanghai can wear
down even the most dedicated urbanite
and those in need of an escape from
the constant din and crowds usually
make a day trip to visit the so-called
water towns located west of the city.
They are quite popular with local
city folk, so it's not really rural, but
the canals crossed by vaulted bridges,
open-air restaurants and large
parks provide a pleasant contrast to
modern Shanghai.

Jiading

Canals ring this pleasant little town in Nanxiang District (known as the home of the Shanghai delicacy called *xiaolongbao*, a sauce-filled dumpling. Aside from the popular canal-boat ride, the town has lovely gardens, including Shanghai's oldest, the Garden of Autumn Clouds, opened in 1502.

17km (10 miles) northwest of Shanghai. Bus: 6A leaves from Shanghai Tiyuchang.

Zhouzhuang

This is the most popular of Shanghai's water towns and dates back to the Warring States period. It's also the most developed. Visitors flock here at weekends and public holidays, but in the week it can be simply delightful. Its narrow, winding streets afford surprises at every corner. The town's boatmen will guide you around the numerous canals and some even sing – you might almost be in Venice.

50km (31 miles) west of Shanghai. Bus: Shanghai Sightseeing Buses leave from Shanghai Tiyuchang from 7am and return by 4pm.

Zhujiajiao

It's quite touristy (although not as much as Zhouzhuang), with shopping malls now encircling the old Ming-era town, but once inside, the canals running through the old town, passing beneath the vaulted bridges, and the canal-side restaurants adjacent are still fun.

Qingpu County, 25km (15 miles) southwest of Shanghai. Bus: Shanghai Sightseeing Buses leave from Shanghai Tiyuchang from 7.30am.

Boats on a canal in the 'water town' of Zhouzhuang

Shanghai environs

There are several major cities and sights surrounding Shanghai worth a visit not only for their historical significance, but also as an oasis of calm after time spent in this busiest of cities. Nearby Suzhou offers some of China's very best gardens, while Hangzhou is often afforded the moniker 'China's most beautiful city'. Nanjing once served as the country's capital and its sad recent history adds a sombre note to any visit. Yangzhou and Wuxi were once prosperous economic centres of Southern China.

Hangzhou

Capital of Zhejiang Province, Hangzhou was also made capital of China in 1127 during the reign of the Song-Dynasty Emperor Gaozong, who was captivated by the beauty of the city's West Lake. It is indeed a pearl beyond price, although in danger of being dulled by too much lakeside development. Just two hours by train from heavily populated Shanghai, Hangzhou can get crowded, and many of its finest sights are immersed in a cataract of noise from tourists and the battery-powered loud hailers used by tour guides. This is sad, because Hangzhou deserves to be savoured. One of the best ways to see the sights around West Lake is to hire a bicycle on Hubin Lu to the east of the lake. Otherwise taxis are the most convenient form of transportation.

Baoshi Shan (Precious Stone Hill)

The most notable feature of the hill is the Baochu Ta (Baochu Pagoda), originally built in the 10th century for the safe return of the Tang Prince Chu, but unattractively restored in the 1930s. The wooded hill overlooks West Lake.
Off Baishan, north shore of West Lake. Tel: (0571) 8717 9617. Open: daily 8am–6pm. Admission charge.

Dayun He (Grand Canal)

The southern terminus of the 1,800-km-long (1,120-mile) Grand Canal can be seen in Hangzhou's northern and eastern reaches, along Huancheng Bei and Huancheng Dong.

Feilai Feng (Peak that Flew from Afar)

The rock formations of this hill, which legend says flew to China from India, are carved with 380 sculptures dating from the 10th to the 14th centuries, of which the most important is that of the Laughing Buddha.
Lingyin, adjacent to Lingyin Si (Temple of Spiritual Retreat).

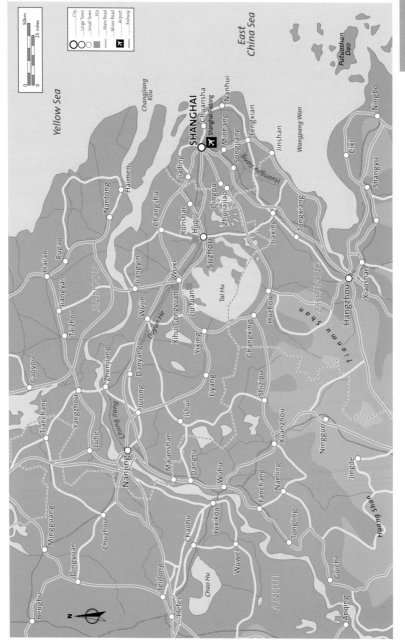

Shanghai environs

Tel: (0571) 8798 8261. Open: daily
8am–6pm. Admission charge.

Huang Long Dong Gongyuan (Yellow Dragon Cave Park)

A pleasant respite from the bustle of
the city, this secluded mountainside
park offers forests of bamboo and
deciduous trees that are alive with
colours in the autumn. All year round
there are quiet pavilions, teahouses and
Taoist retreats. At the summit a small
spring bubbles with water used for
brewing tea which is collected by locals.
The dragon statue here gives the park
its name. Further to the east is Baopu
Daoyuan (Baopu Taoist Garden), an
active centre of worship with monks
chanting Taoist scriptures punctuated
by gongs and chimes. Continue east
and you'll reach Chuyang Tai (Sunrise

Baochu Pagoda on Precious Stone Hill

BOATING ON THE GRAND CANAL

Two boats a day sail between Hangzhou and
Suzhou (*see pp62–7*) as a taste of pre-railway
days when the Grand Canal (*see feature
pp70–71*) was the only viable means of long-
distance transport for both emperors and
ordinary people.

Barges still carry goods on the Grand
Canal, but only tourists move on the water
with leisure. Boats leave from the Hangzhou
Passenger Wharf on Huancheng Beilu, 1km
(¹/₂ mile) east of the long-distance bus station.

Terrace), which offers splendid views
of the lake below.
Entrance on Beishan. Open: 7am–6pm.
Admission charge.

Lingyin Si (Temple of Spiritual Retreat)

Saved from destruction during the
Cultural Revolution only by the
personal intervention of Premier Zhou
Enlai, this beautiful temple dates
originally from 326, although the
structure has been rebuilt many times
since then. A 24-m-high (79-ft)
camphor-wood statue of the Buddha is
the highlight of the temple, located in
the Great Hall.
Lingyin, 3km (2 miles) inland from the
western shore of West Lake. Tel: (0571)
8798 8216. Open: 8am–6pm. Admission
charge.

Qinghefang Gu Jie (Qinghefang Ancient Street)

A lively pedestrianised street re-created
in Qing architecture offering street-side

puppet theatres, traditional medicine shops and a vast array of traditional crafts for sale.

South end of Zhongshan Yan'an.

Xi Hu (West Lake)

First by far among Hangzhou's many attractions is the magnificent West Lake, to the east of which the city has been built. Dozens of scenic spots dot its shores, waters and islands. Many have poetic names, such as Autumn Moon Over the Calm Lake, Three Pools Mirroring the Moon, Solitary Hill and Watching Goldfish at Flower Harbour. Part of the lake's charm is the chance to slip into the poetic appreciation of nature that was once the hallmark of China's leisured classes. Sadly, this is not always possible due to the throngs of visitors and a seemingly inexhaustible supply of noise. Nevertheless, West Lake is just about big enough to find places where visitors can escape for peace and quiet.

Pleasure boats leave from various points on excursions across the lake, which covers about 9sq km (3½ sq miles), and gondolas can also be hired with an oarsman for a slower but more individual appreciation of the sights. The gardens, pools and zigzag bridges of Santanyinyue and Xiaoyingzhou islands (in the western part of the lake) are among the most popular beauty spots.

A causeway connects the biggest island in the lake, Gu Shan, to the shore. On this island one finds the excellent **Zhejiang Sheng Bowuguan**

Serving tea is an art in China

(Zhejiang Provincial Museum. *22 Gushan. Tel: (0571) 8797 1177. Open: Tues–Sun 8.30am–4.30pm. Admission charge)* and the **Xiling Yinshi (Seal Engravers Society**. *31 Gushan. Tel: (0571) 8717 9617. Open: daily 7am–5.30pm. Admission charge)*, which has an interesting display of what we know as 'chops' (stamps or seals). This island and its buildings were once the exclusive domain of the Qing Emperor Qianlong, who used it when he visited Hangzhou.

Zhongguo Chaye Bowuguan (China Tea Museum)

Hangzhou is world famous for its green tea called Dragon Well, in Chinese *long jing*. This museum tells the story of tea quite well, from its history and production methods to the art of serving the tea correctly. Tea gardens surround the museum and continue further up into the hills.

Longjing, southwest of the city. Open: 9am–5pm. Free admission.

Inventions

It seems ironic that so many of China's difficulties with colonial powers in the 19th century were caused by its inferior technology because China has a proud record of innovation stretching back for centuries. Practical and widespread application of the products, however, was lacking.

Gunpowder, the world's oldest explosive, a mixture of sulphur, charcoal and saltpetre, was in use in China as early as the 10th century during the Song Dynasty, when it was used in grenades and rockets, and later in firearms. Another invention, which revolutionised warfare in its time, was the stirrup, which permitted greater power in the delivery of a lance blow.

The crossbow, an even earlier military advance, was first documented in China around the 4th century BC. Sun Tzu's important book *The Art of War* refers to giant crossbows and their use.

Peaceful processes

Paper-making and block printing were more peaceable. Paper was in use by the 2nd century AD, and there are indications that it may have been

The stirrup was a Chinese invention

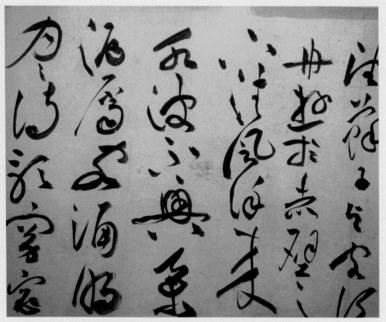

Paper was in use in China long before it was in Europe

invented as early as the 2nd century BC. The earliest-known printed book (AD 868), using the woodblock method, is a Buddhist Diamond Sutra. Although clocks and sundials had been known to people for millennia, revolutionary developments in mechanical clocks using the escapement mechanism came from 11th-century China. The wheelbarrow can be traced to 2nd-century Han Dynasty times and is often seen in tomb murals of that period. The suspension bridge dates to an even earlier time, the 3rd century BC, with examples in both China and Tibet.

The pound lock, used with such success throughout the world's canal systems today, was first developed during the Song Dynasty (960–1279) and put to great effect on the Dayun He (Grand Canal). Piston bellows, developed so enthusiastically during Europe's 18th-century Industrial Revolution, were being used in ancient China as early as the 3rd century BC.

China also gave the world kites, porcelain, the magnetic compass and even a pre-vaccination form of immunisation against smallpox. Then there are noodles, and tea, whose cultivation and consumption began in China.

Shanghai environs

NANJING AND ENVIRONS
Nanjing

Founded in 900 BC, Nanjing, now the capital of Jiangsu Province, has been the capital of China several times and, for some months in 1912, it was the capital of Sun Yatsen's provisional government following the overthrow of the Beijing-based Qing Dynasty. It was also the capital of Nationalist China in 1928–37 and 1945–9. Today, this cosmopolitan city on the southern bank of the Yangzi River has a population of six million.

By any standards, Nanjing is a beautiful city, its tree-lined streets boasting a quarter of a million maple trees and a glorious display of chrysanthemums in autumn. The streets are busy, and the air no doubt is as polluted as anywhere else in China, but it seems less so, thanks to the breezes that sweep along the Yangzi River and down from the surrounding hills. Those hills, especially the Purple and Gold Mountains, are an additional attraction, and their cool air and open spaces make for a fine day out from the city. The best option for getting around widespread Nanjing is by taxi: they are plentiful and inexpensive.

Changjiang Daqiao (Yangzi Bridge)
See two giant bridges for the price of one. The 6.7-km (4-mile) railway bridge is on the lower tier and above

Nanjing

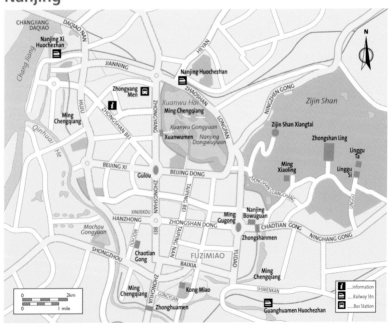

Huge stone elephants guard a path near Ming Xiaoling (the tomb of Hong Wu)

that is the 4.5-km (3-mile) road bridge, crossing the great muddy expanse of the Yangzi. The Chinese are proud of having built these bridges in the 1960s (initially with Soviet aid), as the river had the reputation for being a 'natural moat that is hard to cross'.
Northwest of the city, reached by Daqiao Nan on the right bank and Daqiao Bei on the left.

Chaotian Gong
(Heaven Dynasty Palace)
The Heaven Dynasty Palace was originally a Ming-Dynasty school for the children of high officials, later extended by the addition of a Confucian temple in 1866. Together with other pavilions on the site, such as the Flying Cloud Pavilion and the Imperial Stele Pavilion, they form one of the most perfect monumental ensembles in China. Qing-Dynasty emperors came to the temple to pay their respects to the sage.

Mochou, several blocks east of Mochou Gongyuan. Tel: (025) 8421 9704. Open: 8am–4pm. Admission charge.

Gulou (Drum Tower)
Dating from 1382, the tower displays a 2-m-diameter (6½-ft) drum that was beaten at night to sound the changes of the watch, and an inscribed stone stele mounted on an elephant.
Beijing Xi, at the traffic circle at the intersection with Zhongshan Bei. Tel: (025) 8663 5513. Open: 8am–5.30pm. Admission charge.

Kong Miao (Confucius Temple)
In the atmospheric Fuzimiao district, where shopping, eating and amusements abound, the temple is a symbol of a bygone age. Yet it remains popular with local Chinese, and rightly so. Recently rebuilt, it recreates the atmosphere of its Ming- and Qing-Dynasty heritage, when its role changed from that of imperial educational

establishment to temple. Outside the gate is a canal and a photogenic group of waterside houses.
Gongyuan, off Zhonghua.
Tel: (025) 8662 8639. Open: 8am–9pm. Admission charge.

Linggu Si (Linggu Temple)
Part of the extensive monumental zone beneath the Purple Mountain, this temple was dedicated to Xuan Zang, one of the monks who brought the Buddhist scriptures to China from India. Next to it is the 60-m-high (197-ft) **Linggu Ta (Linggu Pagoda)**, which was designed in 1929 by the American architect Henry Killam Murphy.
Linggu, east of the Sun Yatsen Mausoleum.
Tel: (025) 8444 6443. Open: 6.30am–6.30pm. Admission charge.

Ming Chengqiang (Ming City Wall)
Extensive sections remain of what was once an astonishing 33-km-circumference (20½-mile) defensive wall. Built by 200,000 labourers between 1366 and 1386, the wall averages a height of 12m (39½ft) and a width of 7m (23ft). Some of its 13 gates also survive, including **Zhonghuamen (Zhonghua Gate)** in the south, which has been restored and opened as a museum.

Sections of wall can be seen beside Xuanwu Lake, in the northwest close to the Yangzi River, and particularly in the south, beside the Qinhuai River.

Ming Gugong (Ming Palace)
Little remains of the great palace on which the Forbidden City in Beijing is said to have been modelled. It was

An incense burner in front of the entrance to Linggu Temple at Nanjing

Stone guardian at the Ming Xiaoling Mausoleum

circumference, all inside the city (and rich in carp), it can be toured by motorboat or barge. Children's amusement parks, a small zoo (**Nanjing Dongwuyuan**), pagodas, temples and pavilions can be seen on the tour. The visitors are following an august tradition: Ming- and Qing-Dynasty emperors used the lake for recreation. *Northeast of the city centre, outside the city walls. There are several entrance gates, the main one being Xuanwumen off Zhongyang. Tel: (025) 8361 4286. Open: 8am–8pm. Admission charge.*

destroyed in various waves of rebellion and invasion, and only fragments of it survive today.
Zhongshan Dong, junction of Yudao. Open: 6.30am–11pm. Admission charge.

Nanjing Bowuguan (Nanjing Museum)
Despite its name, this is the provincial museum of Jiangsu, and features an extensive collection of objects from the Stone Age to 1919, including archaeological finds, porcelain and antique astronomical instruments.
4 Chaotian Gong, adjacent to Zhongshanmen. Tel: (025) 8480 2119. Open: 9am–4.30pm. Admission charge.

Xuanwu Gongyuan (Xuanwu Park)
Apart from a series of connected islets and a thin strip around the shore, the park is basically all lake – but what a lake! Some 25km (15½ miles) in

Zhongshan Ling (Sun Yatsen Mausoleum)
Ironically, this is one of the most spectacular monuments in China – ironically, because the revolutionary Dr Sun Yatsen (*see box p58*) was a modest man and a democrat, who would surely be appalled to occupy a tomb so grandiose that even an emperor might have blushed at the sight. Nevertheless, the 8-hectare (19½-acre) site is an impressive monument to the first President of the Republic of China. A series of pavilions and stairways ascends the slopes of the Purple and Gold Mountains (*see listing below*), culminating in the mausoleum, built of dazzlingly white Fujian marble, surmounted by a blue-tiled roof, the whole recalling the Kuomintang (Nationalist) symbol of a white sun against a blue sky.
Zhongshan Guangchang, on the southern slope of Purple Mountain.

Sun's Ming-style mausoleum is as splendid as any imperial palace

Tel: (025) 8443 2799. Open: 8am–5pm. Admission charge.

Zijin Shan (Purple and Gold Mountains)

Overlooking the city, the Purple and Gold Mountains add to Nanjing's green reputation. On the slopes of the mountains is the monumental zone that includes the Sun Yatsen Mausoleum, the Linggu Temple and the tomb of Hong Wu (the Ming Xiaoling Mausoleum). Walking is the best way to reach the summit, but there is also a cable car. Halfway up the pathway, you pass the Zijin Shan Xiangtai (Purple and Gold Mountain Observatory), which is linked to China's space programme. *Northeastern edge of the city, beyond Xuanwu Lake.*

Yangzhou

Northeast of Nanjing lies the historical city of Yangzhou, which experienced great prosperity as the point where the Yangzi River met the Grand Canal. From here, goods from the interior, notably salt and silk, could be transported north to Beijing. Once a city of canals, it now offers splendid religious sights and classical gardens.

Daming Si (Temple of Abundant Light)

Located on a hill northwest of the city, this temple was originally constructed in the 5th century but destroyed during the Taiping Rebellion in the 19th century. The main structure of the temple, the Jian Zhen Hall, was built in

SUN YATSEN

A doctor turned revolutionary, Sun Yatsen (1866–1925) aimed to heal the sickness of China under the weak Qing dynasty, when the country was prey to Western nations bent on conquest.

Born in Xiangshan, in Guangdong Province, he spent most of his life outside China, being educated in Hawaii, then training as a doctor in Hong Kong before practising medicine in Macao. In 1894 he founded the Society for the Revival of China, but had to flee the country after an unsuccessful uprising. Following the rebellion of the United League in 1911, Dr Sun was elected President of the Republic of China but resigned after several months. Civil war ensued. In 1912 he founded the Kuomintang (Nationalist Party) and led it until his death. Dr Sun is widely revered for his Three People's Principles: nationalism, democracy and people's livelihood.

honour of a Chinese Buddhist monk who travelled to Japan in the 8th century, introducing both Buddhism and Chinese culture to the Japanese. While at this temple, try to visit the nearby Pingshan Tang (Pingshan Hall), the opulent home of a Qing-Dynasty governor.
Northwest outskirts of Yangzhou.
Tel: (0514) 734 9720. Open: 8am–5pm.
Admission charge.

Ge Yuan (Ge Garden)

Probably Yangzhou's most renowned garden, it was once the private property of a salt merchant but now is open to the public. Notable for its serene atmosphere and use of bamboo.
10 Yangfu Dong. Tel: (0514) 734 7428.
Open: 7.30am–5pm.
Admission charge.

Shou Xi Hu (Slender West Lake Park)

Yangzhou's most famous sight takes its name from the comparison made with Hangzhou's famous West Lake. A lovely park filled with ornate pavilions and willow-lined walkways, its most notable structure is the Wuting Qiao (Five Pavilion Bridge), commissioned by a wealthy salt merchant in 1757 to commemorate Emperor Qianlong's visit. The park also contains a Tibetan-style pagoda similar to the one found in Beijing's Beihai Park.
28 Da Hongqiao. Tel: (0514) 734 1324.
Open: 6.30am–5pm. Admission charge.

A monk in the Temple of Abundant Light

Yangzhou Bowuguan (Yangzhou Museum)

Located in a former palace of a Ming official, this museum's most notable pieces are a boat that once sailed the Grand Canal and a Han-Dynasty-era jade burial suit.
2 Fengle Sheng. Tel: (0514) 734 4585.
Open: 8am–5pm. Admission charge.

Porcelain

In films, the vase that gets broken by a clumsy guest or a jilted lover is always a priceless piece of Ming – and the fact that it was old somehow does not mollify its owner.

Porcelain

Usually, and appropriately, known as china, porcelain is a hard, thin, vitreous and translucent material, fired at high temperatures (*see below*).

A fine decorative vase

The best porcelain is considered to be as white as jade, as shiny as a mirror, as thin as paper and as resonant as a bell. There are many regional styles, although most can be purchased all over China: Foshan is noted for Shiwan porcelain, Jingdezhen for blue-and-white, eggshell and celadon, Shantou for multicoloured flower motifs, and Yixing for purple-coloured and unglazed wares.

Chinese porcelain, however, has a pedigree stretching back well before the Ming (1368–1644) to the Song Dynasty (960–1279) and earlier (it probably originated in the 6th century). It was unknown in Europe until around 1300, where the earliest imports were thought to be made of some semi-precious material and often set in gold or silver. Not until the early 18th century was its manufacture fully mastered in Europe, at the Meissen works in Germany.

A hard, thin, vitrified and translucent ceramic, porcelain is made from special (feldspathic) clays, whose constituents vary from place to place. It is fired at high temperature, with the glaze being fused to the body. Even today, porcelain is a craft product highly prized by collectors.

Modern reproductions of porcelain originals

It is hand-glazed and fired in kilns whose temperature is determined by the skill of the master potter.

The blues

Blue-and-white porcelain, perfected in the Ming period, was the high point of Chinese porcelain design. The form took Europe by storm, and it continues to do so in such makes as Delft blue. The technique was a complicated one to perfect, and involved painting cobalt on to the clay body before covering it with glaze and firing. Lightness, translucency and delicacy were all achieved by the mid-15th century, and the vessels were highly prized by courts and wealthy individuals around the world.

The isolated town of Jingdezhen, on the Chang River in Jiangxi Province, has long been the porcelain capital of China, thanks to its fine kaolin clay. A Museum of Ceramic History (Taoci Lishi Bolanqu) here illuminates the story, and visits can be made to the town's many kilns where white-glazed, celadon, blue-and-white, overglaze colour and other styles of porcelain are all produced.

SUZHOU AND ENVIRONS

Suzhou, the city of canals and gardens, 85km (53 miles) west of Shanghai, was called the 'Venice of the East' by Marco Polo. An ancient Chinese proverb states, 'In Heaven there is Paradise; on Earth there is Suzhou'. The city's love affair with gardens dates back 2,500 years and continues still. At the time of the Ming Dynasty (1368–1644) there were 250 gardens, of which about 100 survive, although only a few are open to the public.

Tourists can pause in contemplation in these gardens, experiencing nature as the poets, painters and philosophers did, but be sure to arrive before the crowds, who strip the gardens of their calm. Most sights are within short walking distance, but taxis are a cheap option if needed.

The graceful façade of the North Temple Pagoda

The Suzhou area is also famous for Lake Tai, one of China's beauty spots which is threatened by pollution, and further north the Grand Canal town of Wuxi, which faces the lake.

Suzhou
Beisi Ta (North Temple Pagoda)
Nine storeys and 76m (249ft) high, the octagonal pagoda dates from the late 10th century, and though it has been rebuilt several times, it still leans disconcertingly. The view from the top is superb and well worth the exertion. *Renmin, northern sector of the old city. Tel: (0512) 6753 1197. Open: 8am–5.30pm. Admission charge.*

Canglangting Yuan (Blue Wave Pavilion Garden)
Reached by bridge across a brook, the 1-hectare (2½-acre) Blue Wave Pavilion is the only garden not completely enclosed by a wall. In addition, it is the oldest garden in Suzhou, and of a wilder design than the others, with rockeries and artificial hillocks decorated with bamboo. It takes its name from a waterside pavilion built in 1044 by the poet Su Shunqin. *Renmin, between the Nanlin Hotel and the long-distance bus station. Tel: (0512) 6519 4375. Open: 8am–5pm (summer); 8am–4.30pm (winter). Admission charge.*

Huqiu (Tiger Hill)
So named because a white tiger is said to have appeared here during the burial

Musicians entertain at Tiger Hill

of Emperor He Lu in the 5th century BC. The spectacular Tiger Hill Pagoda has tilted dangerously, and has had to be braced to stop it from falling over. *Northwest of Suzhou, 5km (3 miles) from the city. Open: 7.30am–5pm. Admission charge.*

Liu Yuan (Garden for Lingering In)

Plants, trees and rocks abound in this 3-hectare (7¹/₂-acre) garden, including a 6.5-m-high (21-ft) rock which dominates its surroundings. The pavilions are also impressive, including the finely furnished Hall of Mandarin Ducks and the Hall of Trees and Springs, beside the Pool for Watching Clouds. The principal beauty spots are connected by a 700-m (765-yard) corridor. Hundreds of windows latticed in differing floral patterns look out on the rocks, plants and water, giving the effect of pictures at an exhibition viewed through constantly changing frames.

Liu Yuan, northwestern suburbs, beyond the moat. Tel: (0512) 6533 7940. Open: 7.30am–5.30pm. Admission charge.

Suzhou Bowuguan
(Suzhou Silk Museum)

Though fairly small, this informative museum covers Suzhou's history and culture. Exhibits of silk recall the importance of the centuries-old industry to the region.

661 Renmin, near Zhuozheng Yuan. Tel: (0512) 6753 6506. Open: 9am–5pm. Admission charge.

A variety of souvenirs on sale outside the Master of the Nets Garden

Suzhou Shangchang (Suzhou Bazaar)

The 'bazaar' is an attractive shopping and restaurant zone that stands on both sides of the main east–west city centre street (Guanqian), which is itself a pedestrian precinct.

**Wangshi Yuan
(Master of the Nets Garden)**

At just 0.5 hectares (1¼ acres), this is the smallest of Suzhou's gardens, but it compensates with an elegant design that has been widely influential as a model for other Chinese gardens. Courtyards, corridors and pavilions give observation points, and names like the Pine Viewing and Painting Appreciating Hall, and the Moon and Wind Pavilion, convey the flavour of the contemplative hours spent here by the wealthy and leisured former owners. On summer evenings, the garden remains open late and is illuminated with lanterns,

while musicians and folk dancers entertain visitors.

Shiquan, southeastern corner of the Old Town, between the Nanling and Suzhou hotels. Tel: (0512) 6520 3514. Open: 7.30am–5pm. Admission charge.

Xi Yuan (West Garden)

This is actually a Buddhist temple, with gardens attached, dating from the 16th century. Its most notable sight is a series of rooms filled with 500 representations of the Buddha, each with a different character and expression.

Liuyuan, western suburbs, adjacent to Liu Yuan (see p63). Open: 5.30am–7pm (summer); 5.30am–5pm (winter). Admission charge.

Xuanmiaoguan Si (Temple of Mystery)

Considered to be among the finest Taoist temples in China, the Temple of Mystery dates originally from AD 279,

although it was destroyed in 1860 and rebuilt some years later. The great Sanqing Hall, at the heart of the temple, is supported by 60 pillars and topped by a double roof.
Guanqian, Suzhou Bazaar district. Open: 9am–6pm. Admission charge.

Zhuozheng Yuan (Humble Administrator's Garden)

The original garden was gambled away by the son of the 'humble administrator', a former official who laid it out in 1522. The superb ensemble is some 5 hectares (12½ acres) in extent, and one of the finest gardens in China. Water is the main theme here, with the extensive pools overlooked by pavilion-studded banks and dotted with islets reached by graceful bridges or narrow stone causeways.
Dongbei, northeast corner of the Old Town. Tel: (0512) 6753 9869. Open: 7.30am–5.30pm (summer); 7.30am–4.30pm (winter). Admission charge.

CHINESE GARDENS

Most Chinese cities have at least one garden that is worth visiting. Among the more beautiful are Shanghai's Yu Yuan (Yu Garden) and those in and around the West Lake of Hangzhou city, but the finest are to be found in Suzhou. Most city tourist maps list the gardens to be seen.

Shanghai environs

The elegant Master of the Nets Garden

Tour: Suzhou

Few of China's cities are so pleasant to walk around as Suzhou, with its tree-fringed streets, houses built on a human scale, mild climate, and its magnificent gardens. Suzhou is big enough that the distances may be too great for walking all the way. This tour combines walking with taxi and pedicab rides, but if time and energy allow, you will do better just to walk.

Begin at Xi Yuan in the western suburbs.

1 Xi Yuan (West Garden)

Built around a 16th-century Buddhist temple complex and rebuilt in 1892, the gardens feature a pavilion containing no fewer than 500 larger-than-life-sized Buddha images, each of which wears a different expression. A 1,000-arm Buddha guards the entrance.

Cross Huqiu and turn left into Liuyuan to reach the entrance to Liu Yuan.

2 Liu Yuan (Garden for Lingering In)

You will probably want to linger in one of China's most glorious gardens, although not the biggest in Suzhou. Some 200 variously shaped windows look out on to the wooded, floral and watery scene beyond (*see p63*).

You can walk from here, but it is probably best to take a taxi through the Changmen (town gate), along Xizhongshi and Dongzhongshi, then left on Renmin to Beisi Ta.

3 Beisi Ta (North Temple Pagoda)

(*See p62.*)

Continue along Xibei, to Zhuozheng Yuan on Dongbei.

4 Zhuozheng Yuan (Humble Administrator's Garden)

This extensive garden is formed by three connected areas and adds up to an ideal image of the elements that form the traditional Chinese garden: water, rocks, bridges, pavilions, plants and trees, blended into a restful harmony (*see p65*).

Turn into Yuanlin to reach Shizilin Yuan.

5 Shizilin Yuan (Lion Grove Garden)

So named because many of its Lake Tai rocks are shaped like lions in various poses, the garden has a stone boat 'anchored' in its large central lake.

An alternative at this point is to rent a pedicab. Come out on to canal-lined Lindun and turn right into Guanqian.

Stop the pedicab 200m (220 yards) down Guanqian on the right.

6 Suzhou Shangchang (Suzhou Bazaar)

(*See p64.*)
Turn left onto Renmin for Yi Yuan.

7 Yi Yuan (Joyous Garden)

A century old, this is the newest of Suzhou's gardens, formed around a pool crossed by a crooked bridge. *From here, either walk or go by pedicab along Renmin to Canglangting.*

8 Canglangting Yuan (Blue Wave Pavilion Garden)

(*See p62.*)
Retrace your steps along Renmin to Shiquan and continue to the final garden, Wangshi Yuan, reached by a narrow side alley on your right.

9 Wangshi Yuan (Master of the Nets Garden)

(*See p64.*)
It is possible to take a taxi from here back to Xi Yuan and your starting point.

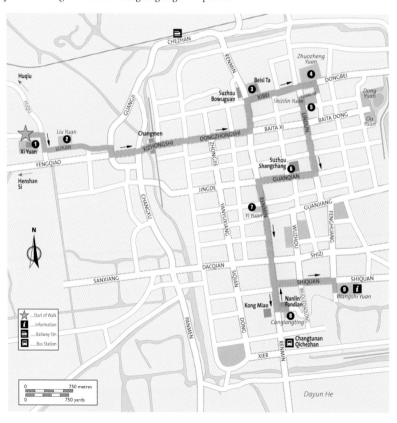

Wuxi

With a history that dates back 3,000 years to the Shang and Zhou dynasties, Wuxi fell on hard times when the tin deposits that gave it life ran out; its name actually means 'no tin'. Although the Grand Canal runs right through it, and the town remains a centre of silk production, Wuxi itself is a smoky industrial centre, and the main points of interest lie some 10km (6 miles) to its southwest, around the shores of Lake Tai.

Dayun He (Grand Canal)

Few places are better situated for watching ordinary life on the Grand Canal than Wuxi. The town's prosperity was a direct result of its position on

Wall shrine in Wuxi

the canal, and barges still maintain a fairly small-scale level of traffic on the water, while old houses with wooden balconies are clustered together on the banks.

There are numerous points of observation, thanks to the city's many bridges, the best being those on Renmin Xi and Liangxi.
Bus: 2.

Li Yuan (Li Garden)

Very nearly in Lake Tai, the garden depends on water for its effect as much as on its trees, pavilions and rockeries. The Lake-Gazing Pavilion looks out over the lake. Dating from 1930, the garden was expanded after 1949. A Stone Boat adds to the nautical flavour.
Hubin, lakeside, east of the Baojie Bridge to Turtle Head Isle. Open: 6.30am–5.30pm. Admission charge. Bus: 820.

Mei Yuan (Plum Garden)

This suffers in comparison with the Li Garden because its pavilions are in a poor state of repair, but the ragged nature of the park may actually be refreshing after the extremely manicured look of most Chinese gardens. Kingfishers dart around the main pool, and a visit early in the year will find the plum trees – symbols of beauty, elegance and endurance – in blossom.
Liangxi, near the Taihu Hotel. Open: 6.30am–5.30pm. Admission charge. Bus: 2.

Tai Hu (Lake Tai)

At 2,235sq km (863sq miles), this is one of China's biggest lakes. Its best-known attribute may not be its fresh waters and the fish they produce, but the big limestone rocks, worn, holed and shaped by the action of wind and water, which are an integral feature of the best Chinese gardens. Lake Tai is a scenic spot of some grandeur, the extensive waters mirroring the hilly shores and dotted with fishing boats, fish farms, junks, pleasure cruisers and islets. Some of the best points have been taken over by tacky amusement parlours and other 'attractions' that cater to local visitors. An exception is the Orchid Conservation and Research Centre, which must be just about unique in China, if only because admission is free!

Most of these attractions are on Yuantouzhu (Turtle Head Isle) – which is actually the tip of the Chongshan Peninsula – and they can be reached by a distinctly shaky monorail within the park, while the rest of the isle is reached by tour boats from Wuxi, or by powerboat from various points along the shore. Tour boats leave from Turtle Head Isle for a short cruise to the Sanshan (Three Hills Isles), an island park that offers superb views across the lake.
10km (6 miles) southwest of Wuxi. Bus: 820 from Wuxi.

Xihui Gongyuan (Xihui Park)

This city park merges with the wide-open spaces of Hui Shan (Hui Hill)

Turtle Head Isle, at Lake Tai, is popular with artists

to provide an airy escape from Wuxi's smog.

On Xi Shan (Xi Hill) stands the Ming-Dynasty Longguang Ta (Dragon Light Pagoda), from whose top a fine view over the city and nearby Lake Tai is in prospect.
Hehui, across the Grand Canal from Renmin. Open: 6am–8pm. Admission charge. Bus: 2.

Dayun He (Grand Canal)

At 1,800km (1,118 miles), the Grand Canal is the longest artificial waterway in the world. It stretches from Hangzhou to Beijing, passing through Suzhou and Wuxi in central China and Shandong and Hebei provinces in the North. Passing through the mountains of Shandong Province it reaches a height of 42m (138ft), its greatest height. The canal's average width is 30m (98½ft).

At present it is not possible to navigate the entire length, but this may change as China takes steps to reopen the canal fully for commerce and tourism.

Originally the brainchild of Fu Chai, the Duke of Wu (present-day Suzhou), and seen as a quick way of transporting troops and supplies north, construction began in the 5th century BC to facilitate the transport of

Parts of the Grand Canal continue to be used some 1,500 years after it was constructed

A traditional fishing boat

rice from the Yangtze Valley to Beijing. During succeeding centuries, rivers and lakes were linked by artificial stretches of waterway to create the whole. The Grand Canal was fully opened in the early 7th century AD and provided the main connection between north and south China.

Since the 10th century, boats travelling along the canal have been able to negotiate the varying elevations along the route by using an elaborate lock system developed during the Song Dynasty.

Although at times it has served as an artery for military adventure, the canal's primary use has been peaceful. During imperial times its main purpose was to transport grain from the southern and central regions to the capital, and at its zenith as many as 8,000 boats conveyed between 250,000 and 360,000 tonnes of grain each year to Beijing.

Silting, combined with the growth of railways, saw the decline of the historic waterway. The canal stayed in use in stretches, and on a smaller scale. In places, houses were built on what had been its bed.

Despite the advent of cruise tourism along the Hangzhou to Yangzhou stretch, this waterway has remained a muddy mess. Yet it traverses beautiful countryside and some lovely cities, offering a glimpse of a time when imperial barges and grain boats plied its route.

Chang Jiang (Yangzi River)

The longest river in China and third longest in the world, the Chang Jiang (Yangzi) is much more than a water course. Known further upstream as the Golden Sand River, it flows through the geographical, spiritual and historical heart of China.

From its source in the Tanggula Mountains of Qinghai Province, the river flows southeast through Tibet as the Tongtian, turns south, then north as the Jinsha, and becomes the Yangzi proper after Yibin in Sichuan. Here, it swings eastwards once again, crossing Hubei, Hunan, Jiangxi, Anhui and Jiangsu provinces to reach the East China Sea at Shanghai. Its source-to-mouth length is 6,300km (3,915 miles).

The Yangzi river basin comprises an area of 1.8 million sq km (695,000sq miles) – a quarter of China's cultivable land – and supports a vast population by providing irrigation and hydro-electric power. The river is also a major transport artery, navigable to ocean-going vessels for 1,000km (621 miles), and to smaller vessels for 3,000km (1,864 miles). It also serves as a convenient drain for the wastes generated along its banks.

The high points of the Yangzi river cruises (*see pp76–7*) are the three gorges, as the wide swathe of the river narrows to hurtle through the gaps between towering cliffs. At 8km (5 miles) in length, Qutang Xia, nicknamed the Windbox Gorge, is the shortest of the three gorges, but it offers a dramatic foretaste of what is to come. Downstream, beyond Wushan, Shennu Peak indicates the start of the 44-km (27-mile) Wu Xia (Wu Gorge), the most spectacular of the three, with six peaks lined up on each side of the river.

After a lengthy interval, the Xiling Xia (Xiling Gorge) heaves into view beyond Zigui. At 75km (46 miles), this is the longest (but also the least impressive) gorge, with rounded hills replacing the earlier jagged peaks.

Chongqing

Chongqing is one of China's most beautifully located towns. It sits at the tip of a narrow peninsula in Sichuan Province, where the Jialing and Yangzi rivers join in a natural amphitheatre formed by the surrounding hills. Sadly, despite its name (meaning 'Double Celebration'), the city does not match the drama of its situation, having been heavily bombed during World War II. Yet it has several points of interest, besides being the starting point for most downriver cruises on the Yangzi.

Chongqing is a huge city with roads twisting and turning everywhere. The bus service is good but unfathomable to all but a local, so the best form of transport is taxi.

Chaotianmen Matou (Chaotianmen Dock)
At the very tip of the peninsula on which Chongqing sits, the dock area offers a busy spectacle of barges and riverside life. Many downriver cruises depart from here.
Northern end of Xinhua & Shaanxi.

Chongqing Bowuguan (Chongqing Museum)
The museum contains remnants from ship burials, Han-Dynasty tombs and dinosaur skeletons found near Chongqing.
72 Zheng, below Pipa Shan.
Tel: (023) 6350 1268. Open: 9am–5pm.
Admission charge.

Pipa Shan Gongyuan (Pipa Shan Park)
From its green eminence, high above the southern part of the Chongqing Peninsula, the park commands a fine view over the Yangzi and the city. While there are some fairly rudimentary amusements and a few teahouses, as well as modern pavilions, Pipa Shan's

Yangzi River (*tour on pp76–7*)

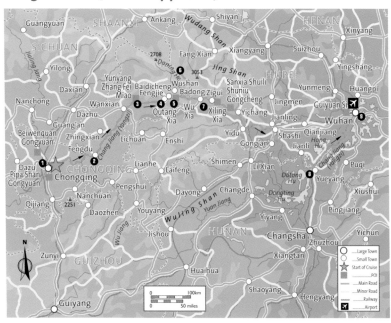

big attraction is the chance it offers to rise above the gritty air of industrial Chongqing.

Zhongshan Er, southwest of the town centre. Open: 6am–10pm. Free admission.

CHONGQING ENVIRONS
Beiwenquan Gongyuan (Northern Hot Springs)

One of two thermal springs complexes near Chongqing, the Northern Hot Springs are set in a landscape of riverside hills. Visitors can bathe either in a public pool or in private chambers. The springs are in a park which also features the Jinyun Si (Jinyun Temple), a Buddhist foundation dating from 1432.

50km (31 miles) northwest of Chongqing in Beibei District. Open: 8am–6pm. Admission charge.

Daning He (Daning River)

The narrow but spectacular gorges of the Daning (*see p77*), a tributary of the Yangzi, are called the 'three lesser gorges', but what they lack in grandeur compared with their cousins on the main river (*see p72*) they certainly make up for in sheer drama. The sight of

A sail boat on the Yangzi

YANGZI MEGADAM PROJECT

In 1919 Dr Sun Yatsen, the founder of modern China, first suggested a dam 'to exploit the water resources' of the Yangzi River.

The megadam, known as the Three Gorges Dam, and located upstream from Yichang, is on a scale that rivals the Great Wall. The dam opened ahead of schedule in 2006. A 658-sq-km (254-sq-mile) reservoir will be created, engulfing the gorges and 30,000 hectares (74,130 acres) of farmland. In the process more than a million residents will be relocated from 300 towns and villages along a 1,000-km (621-mile) stretch of the Yangzi.

There are serious concerns among environmentalists worldwide, who argue against the advantages of big dams, but supporters in China say it will improve flood control and irrigation, as well as supplying 10 per cent of China's total electricity needs.

high-powered boats surging upstream against the current and churning past sections of rapids is not easily forgotten.

Cruise ships stop at Wushan (not to be confused with Wuhan) where passengers transfer to smaller boats to make the four-hour side trip.

Dazu

A scenically situated town 160km (100 miles) northwest of Chongqing, Dazu sits at the centre of one of China's most important Buddhist historical zones. The surrounding area is dotted with 50,000 stone carvings dating from the 9th to the 13th centuries, from the Tang to the Song dynasties. They can be found at 43 separate locations, the main groupings being at Baodingshan and Beishan. The Baodingshan group,

Riding the rapids: heading up the Daning river gorge

15km (9 miles) northeast of Dazu Town, is based around a 12th-century monastery, and was founded by the monk Zhou Zhifeng. His Sleeping Buddha is 31m (102ft) high, and the Goddess of Mercy has 1,000 arms. The biggest single group is at Beishan, 2km (1 mile) north of Dazu. Among the 300 caves sunk into the cliffside there is a sculpture of Wei Junjing, the 9th-century warlord who became a famous stone sculptor.

Wuhan

Most tour boats on the Yangzi begin or end their journey here at the capital of Hubei Province, although some do so at the upstream port of Yichang, or downstream at Shanghai. It's an interesting town in its own right, straddling the Yangzi and Han rivers, with attractive concession-era architecture (yes, the 'Treaty Ports' extended far beyond the coast) along Zhong Shan Avenue in the Hankou District and along Wuluo Road in Wuchang District across the river.

The **Yangzi River Ferry Terminal** (*Yanjiang Dadao, Hankou District. Ticket office tel: (027) 8283 9546.*

Open: 8.30am–5.30pm) on the northwest bank of the river has a number of boats leaving daily for the upriver trip through the Three Gorges to Chongqing.

Guiyuan Si (Guiyuan Temple)

This Buddhist temple dates from the late Ming period and is one of the ten biggest in China, noted for its 500 statues in the Hall of the Five Hundred Luohan, depicting Buddhist holy men. A magnificent jade Buddha image in Southeast Asian style is found in the Cangjing Ge (Sutra Collection Pavilion). The temple is usually busy with worshippers and there is a vegetarian restaurant within the compound. *Cuiweiheng, 3km (2 miles) west of Wuhan. Tel: (027) 8484 1434. Open: 8.30am–5pm. Admission charge.*

Hubei Sheng Bowuguan (Hubei Provincial Museum)

The archaeological collection includes 20,000 items excavated in 1978 from the 2,400-year-old tomb of Marquis Yi, of Zeng in Suizhou, dating from the Warring States period. The tomb yielded a rich treasure of gold, jade and bronze objects, and a fine set of 65 ceremonial bells. Replicas of the bells are played regularly in an impressive performance. A large and relaxing park lies adjacent to the museum. *1856 Dong Hu, beside Dong Hu Mai (East Lake). Tel: (027) 8679 4127. Open: 9am–5pm. Closed: Mon. Admission charge.*

Cruise: Chang Jiang (Yangzi River)

A long, slow, lazy sail along the great riverine artery of central China. Tickets can be bought at Chongqing, or through travel agents either in your home country or in Shanghai. All tour boats follow the Yangzi on its course downstream (see map p73).

Allow two or three days to cover the 1,200km (745 miles).

Begin at Chongqing's Chaotianmen Dock passenger terminal at the peninsula's tip.

1 Chongqing

An unremarkable, even ugly, city occupying a spectacular setting on a hilly peninsula at the confluence of the Yangzi and Jialing rivers, which divides the city in three, Chongqing was the wartime capital of China's Kuomintang (Nationalist) government and suffered heavily from Japanese aerial bombardment. As you leave Chongqing, the riverbank scene gives way slowly from urban to industrial to suburban, and finally to rural, with a hilltop pagoda seen outlined against the city skyline.

The first downstream stop should be at Fengdu.

2 Fengdu Guicheng (Fengdu Ghost City)

Ghost Mountain is the popular name for Pingdushan Mountain, which is dotted with temples and pavilions.

These recall the legend of two men whose names, when joined together, became mistaken for that of the King of Hell, and this reputation clung to the mountain down the centuries. Further on, a pagoda can be seen atop Shibaozhai Rock on Jade Seal Hill. In addition to the rugged scenery along the banks, the river traffic, ranging from tiny wooden junks to seagoing vessels, provides attraction enough. Fishing provides a livelihood for many people along the river.

Open: whenever a boat tour arrives. Admission charge.

The boat should then stop at Wanxian, where harbourside stalls serve meals, and then continues to Yunyang.

3 Yunyang

Yunyang's famous Zhang Fei Miao (Zhang Fei Temple) is lit by multi-coloured lamps at night and the temple's narrow stairways, gloomy natural galleries and legendary statues form a magical and mysterious setting overlooking the river. Market stalls line the steep approach route, and crowds may make the unbalustraded stairways hazardous.

Open: whenever a boat tour arrives. Admission charge. The boat continues to Fengjie.

4 Fengjie

Ancient capital of Kui during the Warring States period, Fengjie is a pleasant enough town that displays little sign of its history now. Continuing along the river and at the mouth of the Qutang Gorge stands Baidicheng, capital of the Western Han Dynasty's 'White Emperor'.

The boat now enters Qutang Gorge, first of the famous Three Gorges of the Yangzi.

5 Qutang Xia (Qutang Gorge)

Varying between 100m and 150m (328ft and 492ft) wide, the gorge funnels river, wind and tour boat into a pell-mell rush between over-hanging hills. This is a very dramatic gorge with a 50-m (164-ft) seasonal variation in depth at this point.

The boat may stop at Wushan, where passengers can transfer to smaller craft for a side trip along the Daning River.

6 Daning He (Daning River)

The Xiao Sanxia (Three Lesser Gorges) of the Daning River are more dramatic than their bigger Yangzi cousins, as the water runs faster and the smaller boats come closer to the rocks and rapids. Some boats will stop at riverside villages if time permits, and this allows for some leisurely walks.

The Yangzi tour boat continues through Wu and Xiling Gorges.

7 Wu Xia (Wu Gorge) and Xiling Xia (Xiling Gorge)

The drama factor continues through these gorges, and the scenery is highly memorable. At the end is the site of the great Yangzi Dam Project, which will eventually drown the gorges and a vast extent of land.

Continue to Yueyang.

8 Yueyang

The Yangzi is a sluggish creature by this time. Some tour boats end their journey here, allowing passengers to connect by rail at Changsha for the south. Yueyang is notable for its Tang-Dynasty Yueyanglou (Yueyang Pavilion) and the vast Dongting Hu (Dongting Lake).

Continue to Wuhan.

9 Wuhan

Most boats finish their trip here, although some continue as far as Shanghai. Wuhan is a big, industrial town notable for its Buddhist Guiyuan Si (Guiyuan Temple), the 1,100-m (3,610-ft) length of bridge over the Yangzi, and the Hubei Provincial Museum (*see p75*).

Wuhan has one of the busiest airports in China and flights can be taken to all major cities in the country.

The southwest

In this chapter we visit the provinces of Sichuan and Yunnan. Sichuan is famed for its cuisine, beautiful mountains sacred to Buddhists, and as the home of China's iconic animal, the giant panda. Yunnan Province gets favourable reviews for its temperate climate, cultural diversity (it is home to 26 of the country's 55 minority nationalities), and remarkable variations in geography, from tropical Xishuangbanna to the Tibetan Plateau in the northwest of the province.

Chengdu

Chengdu is the capital of Sichuan Province, an area of western central China noted for its mild climate, fiery food and the rare and endangered panda. Chengdu's great moment in history passed more than 2,000 years ago: in the 4th century BC it was capital of the Kingdom of Zhou. Chengdu is a large city and you are best to take taxis to and from your destination.

BY TRAIN FROM CHENGDU TO KUNMING

Few rail journeys can match the scenic splendour of the memorable 1,100-km (683-mile), 23-hour trip from Chengdu to Kunming.

As it makes its long, southerly swing through the mountains of Sichuan, the train traverses no fewer than 991 bridges and goes through 427 tunnels. So many splendid views are there that the currency of splendour almost becomes devalued by the repetition of soaring mountains spanning the scenery and reaching into feathery white clouds, and steep descents into green valleys watered by plunging streams.

Renmin Gongyuan (People's Park)

The relaxed ambience and excellent tea served at the lakeside Renmin Chaguan (People's Teahouse) is one of the highlights of this city-centre park. Chengdu is a relatively open and walkable city, but the park is still a welcome escape from traffic and crowds. *Chi Tang, Shi Zhong Xin, southwest of the town centre. Tel: (028) 613 0309. Open: 6.30am–midnight. Admission charge.*

Sichuan Sheng Bowuguan (Sichuan Provincial Museum)

The museum's exhibits cover the life and times of Sichuan, from murals and frescoes taken from ancient tombs, to mementoes recalling the progress of Mao Zedong's Long March through the province. Ming-Dynasty calligraphy and painting is a speciality, and there are some spectacular bronze objects, including a tree with money hidden in the branches.

Renmin Nan, at the junction with Nanyihuan. Tel: (028) 522 2907. Open: 9am–5pm. Admission charge.

Wangjiang Lou Gongyuan (River Viewing Pavilion Park)

Next to the Jin Jiang (Brocade River), the pavilion is dedicated to the Tang-Dynasty poet Xue Tao, who was fond of bamboo, which she regarded as a symbol of modesty and self-control. In her honour, the park hosts a renowned collection of more than 100 bamboo varieties from around the world.

Sichuan University campus, southeastern sector of the city. Open: 6am–7pm (summer); 6am–6pm (winter). Admission charge.

Wuhou Si (Temple of Marquis Wu)

Also known as the Wuhou Temple, this is a wondrously vibrant place, with black-clad monks doing the honours for the marquis, an important statesman of the 3rd-century Three Kingdoms period whose real name was Zhu Geliang.

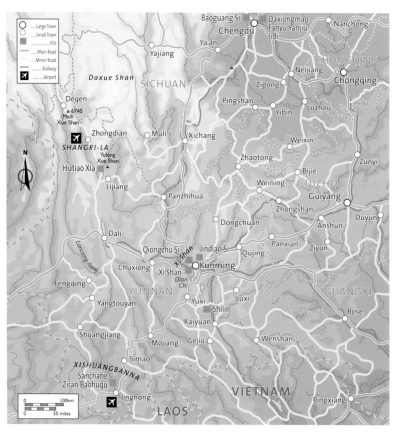

Wuhou Ci Da, adjacent to Nanjiao Gongyuan. Tel: (028) 555 2397/9027. Open: 8.30am–5.30pm. Admission charge.

Chengdu environs
Baoguang Si (Monastery of Divine Light)

There has been a Buddhist monastery on this site for 1,900 years; earlier buildings were destroyed by war, and the present monastery was rebuilt in 1671. Its Tang pagoda has 13 storeys, is 30m (98ft) high and has a pronounced lean. Other marvels are 500 representations of the Buddha, and the carved-stone Thousand Buddha Tablet which dates from AD 450.

Xindu, 18km (11 miles) north of Chengdu. Open: 8.30am–6pm. Admission charge. Bus: from in front of Chengdu's Northern Train Station.

Daxiongmao Fanyu Yanjiu Jidi (Giant Panda Breeding Research Base)

Giant pandas are among the rarest animals on our planet. This incredibly successful breeding centre aims to redress the balance somewhat. Open since 1987, the centre gives the public the chance to see giant pandas of all ages and in greater numbers than anywhere else. It's best to get there early in the morning when the normally sleepy pandas are at their most active. The centre is also home to a number of lesser or red pandas.

26 Xiongmao, 10km (6 miles) northeast of Chengdu. Tel: (028) 8351 6748. Open: 7am–6pm. Admission charge.

Emei Shan

This mountain is sacred to both the Buddhist and Taoist faiths. The highest of three major peaks which form the

Chengdu, like many Chinese cities, combines modern and traditional architecture

A red panda at the Giant Panda Breeding Research Base near Chengdu

summit lies at an altitude of 3,099m (10,167ft). Emei attracts religious pilgrims, seekers of natural beauty and those interested in exotic flora, for over 3,200 plant species thrive here. Fauna-wise, the mountain is notorious for its monkeys. Amusing at first, and holding an important place in Chinese mythology, bands of these beasts have learned that visitors can be intimidated into handing over a free lunch. It's best to carry a walking stick or umbrella to discourage them, and photography is not a good idea, as they're likely to snatch your camera.

A dozen major temples dot the mountain, most of which are recent, and all are active monasteries. These attract the religious pilgrims and are sometimes far from idyllic. The oldest surviving temple is Wannian Si (Long Life Temple) dating from 1611. It

houses a gilded statue of the Buddhist deity Puxian, The Goddess of Universal Benevolence, who Buddhists believe ascended Emei Shan in the 6th century riding a six-tusked elephant. Further up the mountain Jinding Si (Golden Summit Temple) is modern but architecturally impressive and the place from which most people spending the night on the mountain come to see the fabled sunrise.

It takes a serious trekker two full days to reach the summit of Emei Shan, but several cable car routes make it possible to visit as a day trip. There are several small inns on the mountain, and at a pinch you can stay in a monastery. Don't consider this trip in the winter, when the walkways are icy and the weather frigid.

140km (87 miles) southwest of Chengdu. Open: 9am–5pm. Admission charge.

Wildlife

China's wildlife has a hard time. Anything that flies, swims, walks, crawls or slithers is fair game for the cooking pot, and with more than a billion human mouths to feed, much natural habitat has been converted to agricultural use. The exploitative attitude to wildlife has spilled over into other areas, too. Few Westerners will feel comfortable in Chinese zoos, for example, where animals have little space and are often tormented by visitors. Fortunately, this is not the whole story. Large areas of China consist of wilderness or semi-wilderness unsuited to agriculture, where the wildlife, adapted to forest, mountain or desert conditions, can mostly get along quite happily. Nevertheless, habitat destruction for industrial, housing and recreational use continues, while pollution and hunting remain potent threats.

There are certainly fewer wilderness areas in southern China than the northern and western areas of the country, but nevertheless there are some great opportunities for getting

China's endangered species: snow leopards…

out into the wilds and perhaps seeing some rare wildlife. China's first officially protected area, the Dinghu Mountain Nature Reserve, was established in 1956, near Zhaoqing in Guangdong Province. Since that opening, more than 2,000 nature reserves, national parks and other protected areas have been set up by the government. These areas amount to around 14 per cent of the country's land mass. For the visitor some of the best places to visit include Sanchahe Nature Reserve in Yunnan Province, Jianfengling Nature Reserve on Hainan Island and Wolong Nature Reserve in Sichuan Province. Unfortunately, one of the most beautiful protected areas in the country, Huang Shan, not too far from Shanghai itself, was closed to the public in 2007, but is likely to be re-opened in 2010.

...and giant pandas

Endangered species

Not even the star of China's wildlife show, the giant panda, is immune. This symbol of the World Wide Fund for Nature suffers from climate change, habitat loss and reliance on a single food source: bamboo shoots. Fewer than a thousand remain in the wild, mostly in 11 nature reserves in Sichuan Province. The Chinese authorities take stern measures against hunters, including execution, but the survival of this striking black-and-white animal remains in the balance.

Other threatened species include the golden-haired monkey, Père David's deer, the snow leopard, the spotted cat, the pangolin (scaly anteater), the giant salamander and several species of crane. The three species of tiger – the Bengal, South China and Manchurian – are almost extinct. The Yangzi River crocodile and Yangzi River dolphin are both protected species, but that does not stop them being threatened by pollution, sedimentation, fishing nets and collisions with boats.

Birds and greenery make Green Lake Park a favourite outdoor spot

Kunming

The Yunnan provincial capital, with a population of 2 million, styles itself as the 'Town of Eternal Spring', which is only a moderate exaggeration since the altitude (2,000m/6,564ft) and the southern latitude seem to balance each other and create a temperate climate. It is surrounded on three sides by mountains, with Dian Chi (Lake Dian) to the south, which was home to a Bronze Age civilisation well described in the provincial museum. Yunnan's development is more agricultural than industrial (it is the world's biggest rose exporter) so the pollution here is less than in other Chinese cities.

Not quite as big as some of China's other major cities, Kunming's major sights are, however, spread out and the best form of transportation is the very reasonably priced taxis.

Cui Hu Gongyuan (Green Lake Park)

A lovely artificial lake created during the Qing era by channelling water from nearby Lake Dian. Vaulted bridges connect small islands with pavilions, and amateur musicians perform amidst the willow trees.
Cuihu Nan, near Yunnan University.
Open: 6am–6pm. Admission charge.

Nanping Jie (Nanping Walking Street)

In a major urban renewal effort Kunming's former main street was made into a tunnel, creating this pedestrianised street and plaza above. There are recreated Ming-era city gates, whimsical bronze statues, and modern glass architecture.
Nanping, central Kunming.

Shengyi Lu (Shengyi Street)

This middle-class neighbourhood has

elm trees planted on both sides of the street that create a shady canopy. On the left notice a busy flower market, and at the corner of Beijing Lu on the right, a mansion of the mayor during the 1930s, which is now a restaurant. *Shengyi, central Kunming.*

Yunnan Sheng Bowuguan (Yunnan Provincial Museum)

Recently opened after renovations, this three-storey museum has an excellent display of bronze artefacts from the Dian civilisation, which flourished near Kunming around 400 BC, as well as Buddhist art from the Nanzhou and Dali kingdoms. A third gallery holds beautiful jade and gold art objects from the Ming and Qing periods.
Dongfeng Xi, corner of Wuyi. Open: 9am–5pm. Tel: (0871) 364 5655. Admission charge.

Kunming environs
Jindian Si (Golden Temple)

This renowned Taoist temple sits in a scenic location on a forested hill. The present building dates from the Ming Dynasty. In 1695, General Wu Sangui was sent by the new Manchu rulers to pacify the area, but Wu turned against his masters in Beijing. The Golden Temple became one of his palaces.

Made of copper rather than gold, the 6.5-m-high (21^1/$_2$-ft) temple

Drying hay in rural Yunnan

The so-called Stone Forest is formed from eroded limestone rocks

is estimated to weigh 300 tonnes
(295 tons).

7km (4¹/₂ miles) northeast of Kunming.
Tel: (0871) 515 4306. Open: 8am–5pm.
Admission charge. Bus: 10, 71.

Qiongzhu Si (Bamboo Temple)

This Buddhist temple complex contains
a marvellous set of 500 sculpted
Buddhas dating from the 1880s, each
with a different expression and engaged
in some different activity.

12km (7¹/₂ miles) northwest of Kunming.
Open: 8am–6pm. Admission charge.
Bus: minibuses leave from near the
Kunming Hotel (Kunming Fandian) in
Shanghai on Beijing Dong.

Shilin (Stone Forest)

Many visitors travel to Kunming for
no other reason than to visit the
limestone rocks of this so-called
forest. The rocks have been eroded
into fantastical shapes by wind and
rain. Pathways have been constructed
to make things easier, but without a
guide, one can easily get lost in the
maze of paths and miss much worth
seeing. Local Sani minority women,
dressed in traditional costume,
act as tour guides to visitors and
point out the most interesting
rock formations, such as the
Lion Pavilion, Rhinoceros Gazing
at the Moon, Mother and Son

Travelling Together and the Lotus Peak.

120km (75 miles) southeast of Kunming, beyond Lunan Village. Tel: (0871) 771 9006. Open: 9am–6pm. Admission charge. Bus: numerous minibus tours leave from Kunming city centre, departing as soon as they are full.

Xi Shan (Western Hills)

A short drive from Kunming, these hills overlook the city and Lake Dian. There are three major temple complexes in the Western Hills. Travel by vehicle to the terminus of the road near the tomb of the Yunnanese artist Nie Er, who composed China's national anthem, and board a chair-lift to Longmen (Dragon Gate). Here, Taoist monks carved passages through the granite cliffs and built small pavilions with incredible views over the lake far below. A loop through this complex returns you to the point where you boarded the chair-lift. Walk down the main road to Taihua Si (Taihua Temple), an idyllic and little-visited complex dedicated to the goddess Guanyin. In season, camellia and magnolia trees blossom in the gardens. From here there is a surfaced walkway leading through the forest to Sanqing Ge (Sanqing Temple), once the palace of a Mongol prince, now home to fierce monks disallowing photography and tour groups.

10km (6 miles) west of Kunming. Admission charge.

In Yunnan province a villager dries corn in front of his house

The southwest

The Long March

Mao Zedong (1893–1976) led the Communist revolution in China that, in 1949, added one-fifth of the human race to the roster of nations grouped under the red banner. Few individuals match so perfectly with their time and place to have such a major impact on the world. Chairman Mao, the first red emperor of China, born into a farming family in Hunan Province, was one such individual.

Today, Mao's portrait is no longer ubiquitous, and his 'little Red Book', *The Thoughts of Chairman Mao*, is a long way down the bestseller lists, but Mao still commands respect from ordinary Chinese. This is evident in the way the crowds shuffle respectfully past his embalmed body at his mausoleum in Beijing.

After graduating from a teacher training college in Changsha, Mao moved to Beijing where, in 1921, he became a founding member of the Chinese Communist Party. In 1923, the Communists forged an alliance with the Nationalists, and together the 'united front' consolidated power in southern and central China. In 1926, however, the alliance ended in armed conflict and the Communists were driven out of their strongholds. Mao learned two lessons from this: that guerrilla tactics were the way forward; and that 'political power grows through the barrel of a gun'.

Mao memorabilia

Zhou Enlai and Mao Zedong after the Long March

Mao settled in Jiangxi Province, where he set up a series of Soviet bases, but the Nationalists were determined to destroy their former allies. In October 1934, Nationalist forces drove Mao and his followers from the province, and thus began the Long March or, as the Chinese refer to it, the Great March of the Red Army.

Trekking more than 9,500km (5,904 miles) across China, with some 86,000 men, Mao intended to find a new and more secure base in Shaanxi Province from which to pursue his 'people's war'. The epic march, across some of the roughest country on earth, took a year, and only 6,000 of his troops survived. The new base chosen by Mao Zedong, Zhou Enlai and other senior leaders of the Chinese Communist Party was in the remote loess country around Yan'an. Here, the survivors of Mao's First Red Army were joined by survivors of the Second and Fourth Red Armies in a secure base area beyond the reach of Chiang Kaishek's Nationalist forces, themselves increasingly threatened by the advancing forces of Imperial Japan. The Long March was successfully completed in October 1935, and the Communist Party leadership, by now dominated by Mao, began reorganising its forces for the long and successful three-way fight against both the Kuomintang and the Japanese. It was from this secure stronghold in Yan'an that the People's Liberation Army (PLA) would eventually emerge some 14 years later to take control of the entire Chinese mainland and establish the People's Republic of China in 1949.

Lijiang

Lijiang's twisting cobblestone lanes and vaulted stone footbridges crossing rushing canals of clear water, with a backdrop of snow-capped mountains and a rich local culture, have always fascinated visitors. About 160km (100 miles) north of Dali, at an altitude of 2,400m (7,876ft), Lijiang lies at the foot of Yulong Xue Shan (Jade Dragon Snow Mountain), whose towering peaks offer a hint of what awaits further north. The local inhabitants, the Naxi, are a branch of the Tibetan ethnic family who migrated to this fertile terrain 2,000 years ago. Lijiang, a UNESCO World Heritage Site, was devastated by an earthquake in 1995, and the government decreed that all re-building be done in traditional Naxi style. While the Old Town is often full of tourists, it's still possible to wander down the side lanes and escape the souvenir shops.

Heilongtan Gongyuan (Black Dragon Pool Park)

Just north of the Old Town, skirting a small lake fed by an underground spring, which in turn fills the canals of the Old Town, this park features meandering pathways lined by willow and chestnut trees and is home to the splendid Wufenglou (Five Phoenix Hall), built in the 17th century. In the centre of the pool, reached by a gently arching bridge made of white marble called 'the mandarin's belt' or Yudaigiao, is the Deyuelou (Moon Embracing Pavilion), from which one can enjoy a picture-perfect view of the traditional architecture, superb landscaping and the majestic Jade Dragon Snow Mountain.
North end of Xin Da. Open 7am–7pm. Admission charge.

Xishuangbanna

Technically known as the Xishuangbanna Dai Autonomous Prefecture, this southern area of Yunnan is, along with Hainan Island, one of the few areas of China with a tropical climate. It shares borders with Laos and Burma, and has flora and fauna more characteristic of its southern neighbours. The predominant ethnic group, the Dai people, are joined

Early morning view over old Lijiang towards the Jade Dragon Snow Mountain

The enchanting Black Dragon Pool Park, Lijiang

of course by plenty of Han Chinese, but also by other smaller groups such as the Lisu, Yao and Wa, all of which have their own languages and cultural traditions. A visit to any marketplace in Xishuangbanna Prefecture is not only a Tower of Babel, but a kaleidoscope of brightly coloured traditional dress. Xishuangbanna is known for the so-called water-splashing festival, which is in fact the New Year festival of the Dai people. It occurs in the hottest time of the year, mid-April, and is a great way to cool off.

Jinghong, the capital of the prefecture, is not unpleasant but is largely now filled with steel and glass structures that appear out of place here. There are flights from Jinghong to Kunming and even Chiang Mai in Northern Thailand. It is a good place, however, from which to organise trips further afield, including boat trips down the Mekong to Thailand, or overland into Laos. The Burmese border is closed unless you have obtained special permits in Kunming.

Sanchahe Ziran Baohuqu (Sanchahe Nature Reserve)

North of Jinghong is a huge nature reserve (1.5 million hectares/3¾ million acres), part of which has been opened to tourism. There is a chair-lift that passes above the tropical forest canopy, with both wild and trained elephants, and a World Wildlife Federation-sponsored ecotourism project detailing birds and butterflies indigenous to the area. It's even possible to spend the night in a treehouse in the reserve. *About 50km (30 miles) north of Jinghong. Tel: (0691) 243 0299. Open: 9am–6pm. Admission charge. Bus: all buses from Jinghong to Simao and on to Kunming pass the reserve.*

Development vs the environment

All major industrial powers in history have achieved their success at the expense of the environment, placing development before environmental concerns. Britain, the USA and Japan all polluted their way to prosperity and began the clean-up only when the middle classes created by industrial development demanded clean air and water. Sometimes the efforts came too late – the London killer fog of December 1952, caused by coal smoke, remains the biggest single environmental disaster of modern times. China is following this ignoble path but with a significant difference – while the pace of economic development (and the attendant pollution) is unprecedented, large segments of the population still live in poverty. Add to this the worldwide concern over the global warming phenomenon, and the problem is truly staggering in scope.

No visitor to China will be surprised to learn that 16 of the world's 20 most polluted cities are in China, or that only 1 per cent of the urban population breathes air considered safe by international standards. Water-borne pollution is just as serious, with major lakes now unfit even for agricultural irrigation and much of the sea coast red with algae, which kills all marine life. By most counts, China became the world's

Coal-fired power plants are mostly responsible for pollution in China

Pollution over the Bund, Shanghai

biggest polluter in 2007. The airborne pollution from China spreads not only over Asia, but as far away as the USA.

As in 1952 London, the culprit for air pollution is coal. China relies on its abundant coal supplies for its energy needs and uses more coal than Europe, Japan and the USA combined. The heavy industries, such as steel and cement making, that have propelled growth, run exclusively on coal-fired power plants. Sadly, the country is choking on its own success.

China's government is painfully aware of the problems and is making efforts to change the practices that are polluting the country. The much-maligned Three Gorges Dam is only one of many hydro-electric dams under construction. The 'development first' policies of the Deng era are being scaled back somewhat, as government-controlled prices for water and electricity are raised, but the authorities also fear 'social instability' (a polite way of saying a massive revolt against the Communist Party), which would result if the economy cooled dramatically and cost workers their jobs. On the other hand, there have been many instances of local protests by villagers outraged by polluting factories. There is truly no easy solution to the problem.

The south

The south includes the southern provinces of Fujian, Guangdong, the inland Guangxi Autonomous Region and the island of Hainan, the country's smallest province, which is commonly known as 'China's Hawaii'. As the men of Guangdong and Fujian have for centuries been China's greatest seafarers and émigrés, the area, particularly through its cuisine, is well known to foreigners. It was also where Deng Xiaoping first chose to develop centres of free enterprise.

All the capitals and large towns within these provinces are well connected to Shanghai, Beijing and Hong Kong either by new airports or by well-established bus and rail links.

FUJIAN PROVINCE
Xiamen

Considered by many to be the most attractive city in Fujian Province, Xiamen has a colourful history and has preserved its cultural artefacts well. Known in the West as Amoy, the first foreigners to settle here were the Portuguese. The favourite local son is General Koxinga who fought an ultimately futile battle to return power to the indigenous Ming Dynasty from the usurping Manchu Qing rulers.

Xiamen is an island, connected to the coast by a 5-km (3-mile) causeway. Just off the coast lies another island, Gulang Yu, a car-free zone and once a foreigner-only enclave, and a few miles further out to sea lies Jinmen Island, which is claimed by Taiwan. The liveliest part of Xiamen is along the waterfront facing Gulang Yu. It's a bustling seafront with concession-era architecture and good seafood restaurants.

Gulang Yu Island

A ten-minute ferry ride takes you to this islet (2.5sq km/1sq mile) with not a car around – although some battery-powered golf carts are permitted. The architecture and atmosphere is European, and crooked lanes meander through residential neighbourhoods. At the south end of the island a statue of

View of Xiamen from Gulang Yu Island

the local hero Koxinga gazes out to sea. He not only defended Xiamen from the Qing for a good while, but also ousted the Dutch from Taiwan. The main tourist attraction on Gulang Yu is **Xiamen Haidi Shije (Xiamen Seaworld),** an aquatic theme park (*Tel: (0592) 206 7668. Open: 8.30am–8pm. Admission charge*).

Huli Shan Paotai (Huli Shan Fort)
This hilltop fortress still has cannons of German manufacture (dated 1891) pointed seaward. Below the fortress lies the leafy campus of Xiamen University, and next to the campus lies Xiamen's most interesting Buddhist temple, Nanputuo. *Daxue, southern Xiamen. Open: 9am–5pm. Admission charge.*

GUANGZHOU
Guangzhou (Canton)
The capital of Guangdong Province is among the fastest-growing cities on earth in terms of population and

wealth. The town is located in the Zhujiang Hekou Sanjiaozhou (Pearl River Delta), close to Hong Kong, Macao and their adjacent special economic zones. Western investment has flowed into the city from these capitalist neighbours, and the Cantonese, with their characteristic flair for business, have been quick to take advantage. On the downside, Guangzhou is busy, hot, preoccupied

with making money, and is a magnet for unskilled peasants from the countryside migrating in search of a good life that many will never find.

**Guangdong Sheng Bowuguan
(Guangdong Provincial Museum)**
This museum is split between two buildings. The old building contains items pertinent to the life of Lu Xun (1881–1936), one of modern China's

Guangzhou

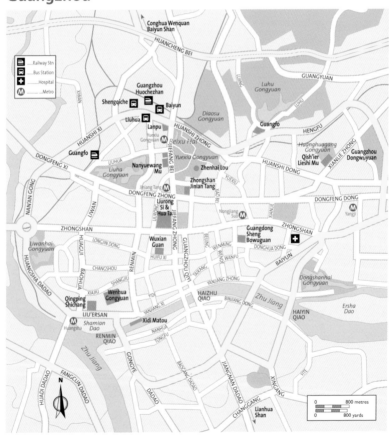

Popular culture: dragons in Guangzhou

greatest writers. The newer building's exhibits include some interesting archaeological objects, tools and pottery from the Guangzhou region.
215 Wenming, north of the Pearl River. Tel: (020) 8383 8432. Open: 9am–5pm. Admission charge. Metro: Nongjiang Suo.

Guangzhou Dongwuyuan (Guangzhou Zoo)

One of the largest in China, this zoo houses some 200 species, including rare animals such as pandas.
Xianlie Zhong. Tel: (020) 8775 5269. Open: 8am–5pm. Admission charge. Metro: Yangji. Bus: 11, 65.

Huanghuagang Qishi'er Lieshi Mu (Mausoleum of the 72 Martyrs)

This monument and park honours the first violent and unsuccessful attempt, in April 1911, to overthrow the Qing Dynasty and drag China into the modern world. A later insurrection the same year was successful, and the monument was built in 1918 to commemorate the earlier effort. Chinese people from around the world contributed to the cost, and had their names inscribed on the monument. A miniature representation of the Statue of Liberty symbolises the kind of democratic ideals espoused by Sun Yatsen and his followers, but lost sight of in the subsequent rise to power of the Communist Party.
Xianlie, on Huanghuagang (Chrysanthemum Hill). Open: 9am–5pm. Admission charge. Metro: Yangji. Bus: 11, 65.

Serene Buddha statues inside the Six Banyan Temple

Liurong Si & Hua Ta
(Six Banyan Temple & Flower Pagoda)

Refreshingly, this temple is often filled with worshippers, and monks chant here on several mornings a week. The building takes its name from six banyan trees celebrated by the Tang-era poet Su Dongpo in the 10th century. The trees are no longer there. What remains is the nine-storey Hua Ta (Flower Pagoda), almost 58m (190ft) high, from which a superb view can be had over the old city.

Liurong, town centre, west of Jiefang Zhong. Tel: (020) 8339 2843. Open: 8am–6pm. Admission charge. Metro: Jiniang Tang.

Qingping Shichang
(Qingping Market)

This big, shambolic and, for animal lovers at any rate, potentially distressing market has become a tourist attraction in its own right since its opening in 1979 (although less so since 2003, as SARS may have originated here).
Qingping & Tiyun, off Liu'ersan. Open: 8am–6pm. Metro: Huangsha.

Wenhua Gongyuan (Cultural Park)

Sports and funfair attractions are featured in this popular centre which defines 'culture' very broadly. Chinese opera is occasionally performed here in full costume.
37 Xi Ti Er Ma, off Liu'ersan, north of Shamian Island, near Renmin Qiao. Tel: (020) 8188 2488. Open: 8am–6pm & for performances. Admission charge. Metro: Huangsha.

Yuexiu Gongyuan (Yuexiu Park)

This 93-hectare (230-acre) park features the Beixu Lake, where rowing boats can be hired, a swimming pool and other sports centres. The park also contains several monuments. These include the 28-m (92-ft) Zhenhai Lou (Zhenhai Tower), which once formed part of the city wall and now houses a branch of the Guangdong Museum, a sculpture of five rams representing the legend of Guangzhou's foundation by five gods who descended from heaven on rams to bring rice to the city, and the Sun Yatsen Monument, a granite obelisk dedicated to the founder of the Chinese Republic, erected in 1929. Across Jiefang Bei Road at the front gate of the park is the Lanpu (Orchid Garden), with 10,000 examples of different orchid species.
Jiefang Bei, adjacent to the China Hotel. Tel: (020) 8669 0556. Open:

6.30am–8pm. Admission charge.
Metro: Yuexiu Gongyuan.

Zhongshan Jinian Tang
(Sun Yatsen Memorial Hall)

With seating for almost 5,000 people, this impressive theatre and cultural centre, set in spacious grounds, was built in honour of the mild-mannered revolutionary, Dr Sun Yatsen, who brought down the curtain on 5,000 years of imperial rule, and initiated Republican government, in 1911.

The hall hosts performances of music, theatre, Chinese opera and dance.

Dongfeng Zhong, north of the town centre. Tel: (020) 8355 2430. Open: 6am–9pm & for performances. Admission charge. Metro: Jiniang Tang.

Granite rocks encased in lush greenery provide a spectacular environment for walking enthusiasts at Lotus Mountain

CRUISING ON THE PEARL RIVER

As well as arriving in Guangzhou by boat, it is possible to make daytime and evening excursions on the Pearl River to view the fascinating life on the water, as well as the city's skyline. These leave from Pier No 1, on the eastern side of Renmin Bridge and, in the evening, from nearby Pier No 2 and from Shamian Island.

Guangzhou (Canton) environs
Baiyun Shan (White Cloud Hills)

These green, lake-dotted hills, partly accessible by cable car, are a popular rambling and dining location with the Cantonese. Moxing Ling (Star Touching Hill) is the highest. Although its summit is at the less-than-dizzy altitude of 380m (1,247ft), it still provides an extraordinarily fine view over the city and the Pearl River delta.

15km (9 miles) north of Guangzhou. Tel: (020) 8722 9871. Open: 8am–7pm. Bus: 24 from People's Park.

Conghua Wenquan
(Conghua Hot Springs)

The mineral springs resort of Conghua lies near the town of the same name. The temperature of the hottest spring is 70°C (158°F), and you can swim in or drink the waters in numerous hotels – the perfect way to cure the aches and pains induced by touring China.

The resort is 16km (10 miles) from Conghua, and can be reached by bus or taxi from Conghua. Open: 8.30am–4.30pm. Admission charge.

The south

Chinese medicine

During the Ming Dynasty, female herbalists – reputed to be witches – from Guizhou Province in southwest China are said to have concocted a wicked brew that could entrap men in matrimony. Today, most herbalists are engaged in the far less sinister task of trying to cure the everyday afflictions of the human

As in all traditional societies, herbalists and alternative practitioners use a variety of ingredients to effect their cures

condition such as haemorrhoids, impotence, insomnia, eczema and even old age.

Guizhou remains at the centre of the Chinese medical world and is the source of many medicinal plants that grow abundantly in its hills, forming the basic ingredients of a medical revolution. From Guizhou comes a cure for haemorrhoids that involves dissolving a herbal powder in water and sitting in it for 30 minutes while the problem vanishes. It seems too good to be true, and it probably is, yet the market for this and other cures is booming. One Guizhou company reportedly makes around US$30 million a year selling herbal sperm regeneration powders and herbal aphrodisiacs, while it is playing the other side of the procreation market by trying to develop a herbal contraceptive.

The alternative way to health

Traditional Chinese medicine has a 2,000-year legacy and is favoured by a quarter of humanity for its supposed efficacy. The first official pharmacopoeia was produced in AD 659. New 'traditional' medicines are being added to the doctor's

Herbs are at the heart of Chinese medicine

armoury all the time. Unfortunately, some of the alternative medicines rely heavily on animal products. Today, organisations like World Wide Fund for Nature (WWF) are working with traditional Chinese medicine practitioners to encourage them not to use the bones and horns of endangered species such as tigers and rare deer.

Acupuncture, in which needles are inserted at key nerve centres in the skin, and reflexology are among the better-known techniques and are said to be effective against a wide range of conditions, including rheumatism, travel sickness and the common cold. Chronic ailments are often treated with herbal remedies, said to have fewer side-effects than Western-style drugs, and simple complaints like colds can be ameliorated in the same way. For acute conditions, especially those requiring surgery, modern techniques are likely to be more reliable.

Lianhua Shan (Lotus Mountain)

Not much of a mountain, really, but a fascinating and idyllic place nonetheless (except at weekends, when the crowds are out in force). This used to be a stone quarry, and weathered holes in the granite indicate where the stonemasons acquired the most impressive pieces. It became fashionable to inscribe calligraphy in the stone, and now gardens, lotus-filled pools and viewing pavilions have been added to create a memorable stroll.
Located some 40km (25 miles) southwest of Guangzhou, and reached by bus or boat. Tel: (0755) 8306 7950. Open: 8am–8pm. Admission charge.

THE GUANGXI AUTONOMOUS REGION
Guilin

Located in the Guangxi Autonomous Region, Guilin has become one of the country's most visited towns, thanks to its setting in a landscape of limestone hills thrust up from the sea bed 300 million years ago and immortalised in Chinese painting and poetry. The city itself, although pleasantly situated on the banks of the Li River and an attractive enough place for walking in, is busy, and its attractions are not quite as memorable as they are often made out to be.

Diecai Shan (Folded Brocade Hill)

The twin peaks of the 73-m-high (239-ft) hill are named Guangyue Shan (Bright Moon Peak) and Siwang Shan (Seeing Around the Hill). Both offer views of the city and the river. The Feng Yan (Wind Cave) en route to the top has Ming- and Song-era poetry inscribed on the walls, and Buddhist sculptures, some of them damaged by the Red Guards.
Diecai, overlooking the river north of the centre, west bank. Tel: (0773) 282 2762. Open: 8am–6.30pm. Admission charge.

Traditional boats on the Li River

Celebrated in Chinese painting, the hills of Guilin

Ludi Yan (Reed Flute Cave)

The stalagmites and stalactites of this cave are magically lit, and present an extraordinary underground vista. The great limestone galleries lead to petrified accretions that have adopted fantastic shapes over the millennia. All have names, and some of them are clearly as described, while others are fanciful or depend on poetic licence. *Ludi, at Yujiazhang, several km outside town, to the northwest. Tel: (0773) 282 2254. Open: 8am–4.40pm. Admission charge. Bus: 3 from Guilin railway station.*

Qixing Gongyuan (Seven Star Park)

The park gets its name from its peaks being aligned more or less in the same configuration as the stars of the Plough in the Ursa Major (Great Bear) constellation. Adjacent to the park are stone stelae (standing stones) carved with calligraphy at the Guilin Beilin Bowuguan (Guilin Forest of Stone Inscriptions).

BOAT TRIP ON THE LI RIVER

There can be no better way of viewing the stunning limestone hills around Guilin than from the deck of one of the small cruise boats that make the eight-hour journey from the city downstream to Yangshuo (although if time permits, going there by mountain bike is also good). The boat offers a close-up view of the strange rock formations that give this area a feeling of 'the land that time forgot'. Life on the river is equally fascinating, with fishermen on bamboo rafts using cormorants to bring in their catch. Traders on flimsy rafts manoeuvre alongside the rapidly moving excursion boats in a dangerous sales tactic, offering fruit and t-shirts.

The giant Guanyin statue near Sanya on Hainan Island

Ziyou, east bank of the river, beyond Liberation Bridge. Tel: (0773) 581 4342. Open: 8am–5pm. Admission charge.

Xiangbi Shan (Elephant Trunk Hill)

A much-photographed riverside rock formation at the junction of the Li and Yang rivers, this looks like an elephant drinking water.

Wenming, beside the river on the west bank, south of the town centre. Tel: (0773) 282 5844. Open: 8am–5pm. Admission charge.

Yangshuo

Yangshuo is where cruises down-river from Guilin finish. The town has the same advantages as Guilin, in terms of its location among the limestone hills, but largely without the hassle, hype and overcharging of that city.

The Yangshuo waterfront, however, is a noisy tourist trap of souvenir stalls and photogenic cormorant fishermen who want payment for pictures taken. Away from the riverside, the village lives up to its 'more genuine' reputation, and is a good place for strolling around.

On the Li River, some 80km (50 miles) south of Guilin. The bus from Guilin takes less than 2 hours.

HAINAN

China's largest island and smallest province has gone from a place of exile for disgraced officials and political dissidents to a tropical resort where residents of China's less temperate zones bask on the beaches far from their snowbound home provinces. While the beaches are lovely, quite a few others will be sharing the experience with you, and those seeking something more tranquil should explore the verdant interior of the island, where the indigenous Li people and other minority groups live. The provincial capital of the island, Haikou (population 2 million), lies at the north of the island.

The beaches

The beaches are located on the southeast coast of the island. The most famous is the recently manufactured town of Sanya, with dozens of resorts, a raucous nightlife scene, and good seafood restaurants. It's great for people-watching, and if you get away from the central area the beaches become less crowded. Yalong Wan (Yalong Bay) is just west of Sanya and is home to the most exclusive resorts on the island. Northeast of Yalong are the less popular Shimei Wan (Shimei Bay) and even quieter Riyue Wan (Sun and Moon Bay).

Sanya is 300km (186 miles) southeast of Haikou and has its own airport.

The highlands

A good alternative to the beaches is a trip into Hainan's cool central highlands. **Wuzhi Shan (Wuzhi Mountain)** is sacred to the local Li people who live in this area. The town of **Tongshi** is quite relaxed, has good accommodation, and treks and visits to minority villages can be arranged here. *223km (139 miles) southwest of Haikou & 90km (55 miles) northeast of Sanya.*

A beachside restaurant on Hainan Island

Hong Kong and Macao

Formerly a British Crown Colony, Hong Kong, this fast-paced special administrative area, has one of the world's most vibrant economies. It lies off the southeastern coast of China and consists of Hong Kong Island, Kowloon and the New Territories, along with some 230 islands and islets. Macao lies some 60km (37 miles) west of Hong Kong. Its territory includes the islands of Taipa and Coloane, which are reached by bridge from Macao town. Regular buses and minibuses run between all of Macao's islands.

HONG KONG

On 1 July 1997, Hong Kong returned to Chinese rule, ending a connection that went back to 1841, when Britain seized Hong Kong Island, it being formally ceded the following year. In 1860, the mainland territory of Kowloon was also ceded to Britain, and in 1898, the New Territories, Lantau Island and other outlying islands were leased for 99 years. China's 'one country, two systems' proposal should allow Hong Kong a large degree of independence in domestic affairs. Its free port and customs status is being retained, and the Hong Kong dollar (HK$) remains the official currency.

With a population of over 7 million living in just over 1,000sq km (386sq miles), it is notoriously densely populated. Just northeast of the territory is the booming Shenzhen Special Economic Zone, created as a part of China's plan to benefit from Hong Kong's economy.

Hong Kong has a very efficient Mass Transit Railway (MTR) which serves almost all areas of the territory. Ferries run between islands and also criss-cross Victoria Harbour to all points.

Hong Kong Island

The attractions of the island are endless. Hong Kong's financial centre is here, along with an antiques and curios district, ferry terminals for the islands, beaches and coastal resorts, the Wanchai nightclub area, Victoria Peak (reached by a hillside tram), and some fabulous shopping, dining and entertainment possibilities. Getting about is easy using either the bus system or the metro (known as the MTR, the Mass Transit Railway).

Bays and beaches

The island's south coast is dotted with resorts and some fine beaches, although the resorts can be pretty crowded, and typical Hong Kong tower blocks are never far from view. In addition, the

Hong Kong and Macao

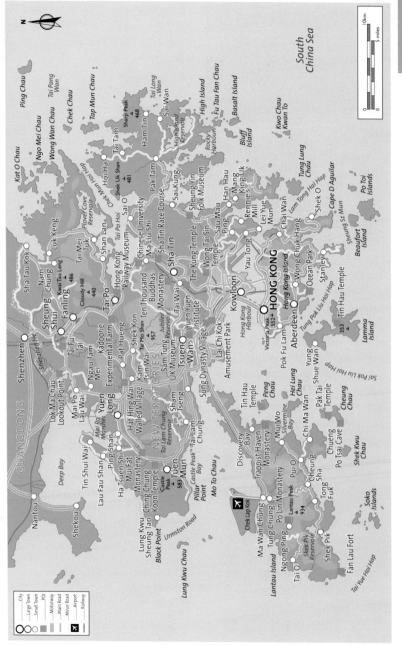

South China Sea

N

0km
0   5 miles

Legend:
- City
- Large Town
- Small Town
- POI
- Motorway
- Main Road
- Minor Road
- Airport
- Railway

GUANGDONG

Shenzhen

Nantou

Shekou

Deep Bay

Tin Shui Wai

Lung Kwu Sheung Tan
Black Point
Lung Kwu Chau

Pillar Point

Urmston Road

Mo To Chau

Lok Ma Chau Lookout Point
Mai Po Marshes
Mai Po
Lau Wai
Yuen Long
Ha Tsuen Shi
Ping Shan
Mui Fat Monastery
Ching Chung Koon Temple

Tuen Mun
Castle Peak 583

Sha Tau Kok

Sheung Shui
Nam Chung
Fanling
Luk Keng

Tai Fu Tai

Kat O Chau

Ngo Mei Chau
Wong Wan Chau
Tai Pang Wan
Chek Chau
Tap Mun Chau
Ping Chau

Shenzhen Hui
Kwai Tau Leng 486
Cloudy Hill 440

Kadoorie Experimental Farm
Ngau Tam Mei
Hat Hing Wai Walled Village
Pat Heung
Shek Kon
Tai Mo Shan 957
Kam Tin
Tsin Wai
Sham Tseng
Tai Lam Chung Reservoir

Tai Mei Tuk
Shan Lan
Plover Cove Reservoir
Tai Po
Hong Kong Railway Museum
Sai O
Shek Uk Shan 481

Tai Tam
Ham Tin
High Island
Highisland Reservoir
Sharp Peak 468
Tai Long Wan
Sai Wan
Wong Tai Sin Temple
Hoi Ha
Pak Tam
Chek Mun Hoi Hap

Ten Thousand Buddhas Monastery
Jubilee Reservoir
Yuen Yuen Institute

Chinese University
Ma Liu Shui
Sha Tin Race Course
Sha Tin
Sai Kung
Sheung Yiu Folk Museum

Fu Tau Fan Chau
Basalt Island
Rocky Harbour
Bluff Island
Kwo Chau Kwan To

Tai Lung
Chau

The Kung Temple
Sau Mau Ping
Han Hau
Mang Kung Uk
Rennie's Mill
Lei Yue Mun
Chai Wan
Wong Chuk Hang
Lam Tong Hoi Hap
Shek O
Cape D'Aguilar
Po Toi Islands

Kowloon

HONG KONG
Hong Kong Island
Victoria Peak 552
Hong Kong Harbour

Aberdeen
Ocean Park
Stanley
Tin Hau Temple
Tung Pok Liu Hoi Hap

Lamma Island

Beaufort Island
Sheung Sz Mun

Lai Chi Kok Amusement Park
Tsuen Wan
UK Museum
Sung Dynasty Village
Sam Tung
Tseng

Tin Hau Temple
Peng Chau
Hei Lung Chau

Pok Fu Lam
Yung Shue Wan
Pak Tai Temple
Cheung Chau
Chuen
Po Tsai Cave
Shek Kwu Chau

Discovery Bay
Silvermine Bay
Mui Wo
Chi Ma Wan
Cheung Sha

Trappist Haven Monastery
Pui O

Ma Wan Chung
Tung Chung
Po Lin Monastery
Ngong Ping
Tai O
Lantau Peak 934
Shek Pik Reservoir
Shek Pik
Fan Lau Fort
Lantau Island

Chek Lap Kok

Tong Fuk

Soko Islands

Tai Yue Hoi Hap

Sai Pok Liu Hoi Hap

NEW TERRITORIES

Lau Fau Shan

A modern building on Lantau

water is polluted enough to make one think twice about stepping into the invitingly azure sea. The fishing port of Aberdeen, with its junk-crowded harbour and floating restaurants, is a picturesque sight, and nearby are the Ocean World aquatic theme park, the beaches of Repulse Bay and the coves of Stanley, also noted for its market.

The south coast resorts and beaches are reached by bus from the underground station at Exchange Square, between the Star Ferry and the Vehicular Ferry Pier.

Fung Ping Shan Museum

This museum contains a good display of Chinese art, organised chronologically so that it acts as a good introduction to the bronze, ceramics and painting exhibits. There is also a very unusual collection of bronze crosses from the Yuan Dynasty (1279–1368).

94 Bonham Road, University of Hong Kong. Tel: (0852) 2241 5500. Open: Mon–Sat 9.30am–6pm, Sun 1.30–5.30pm. Free admission. Bus: 3 to Bonham Road.

Hong Kong Park

This beautifully designed oasis of green has fountains and pools, an aviary, a greenhouse, a visual arts centre, an amphitheatre and tai chi exercises in the mornings. In addition, there is all-important shade and fragrant air. The excellent **Flagstaff House Museum of Tea Ware** is located inside the park.
Main park entrance on Supreme Court Road. Tel: (0852) 2521 5041. Open: 7am–11pm. Free admission.
Museum of Tea Ware. Tel: (0852) 2869 0690. Open: 10am–5pm. Closed: Wed. Free admission. MTR station: Admiralty.

Man Mo Temple

Dedicated to an unlikely combination of the calligraphy-creating God of Literature and the sword-bearing God

LANTAU

Lantau, Hong Kong's largest island (larger, in fact, than Hong Kong itself), lies an hour away by ferry from Central district. The ferry calls at several smaller islands before reaching the main Lantau Harbour at Mui Wo (Silvermine Bay). Lantau is a weekend retreat. Hong Kongers go to climb the 934-m (3,064-ft) Lantau Peak, visit Po Lin (Precious Lotus) Monastery, with its 34-m-high (111-ft) statue of the Buddha, or to explore Tai O, a fishing village on stilts. There is now a new airport on an island off Lantau's northern coast.

of War, this large Taoist temple is an important religious foundation dating from the early years of British rule. It's situated next to the steeply rising staircase of Ladder Street.
124–126 Hollywood Road, Mid-Levels. Tel: (0852) 2540 0350. Open: 6am–6pm. Free admission. MTR station: Sheung Wan. Bus: 26.

Tai Ping Shan Street

With its old temples and ancestral halls Tai Ping Shan Street retains the feeling of traditional, old Hong Kong Island. The Kwun Yam Temple (No 34) is devoted to the Goddess of Mercy and further down the street (No 42) is the Pak Sing Ancestral Hall, filled with ancestral tablets to the dearly departed.
Tai Ping Shan Street, Sheung Wan. MTR station: Sheung Wan. Bus: 26.

Victoria Peak

The spectacular view of Hong Kong from the top of Victoria Peak would be reason enough to make the journey, but getting there by the Peak Tram railway makes the experience doubly entertaining. Once there, a curious fountain with dancing water-jets and an upmarket shopping gallery are about the only attractions, although you can follow the tarmac-covered path for dizzying views in every direction.
Peak Tram Station. 33 Garden Road, Central (adjacent to the US Consulate). Tel: (0852) 2849 7654. Peak Tram operates 7am–midnight. Ticket charge.

Kowloon

Kowloon occupies the southern tip of the Chinese mainland, facing Hong Kong Island's northern shore.
(continued on p112)

Junks in Aberdeen Harbour, on the south side of Hong Kong Island

One country, two systems

On 1 July 1997, in a ceremony charged with emotion, China resumed sovereignty over what had been for the previous 156 years the British Crown Colony of Hong Kong. To the Chinese government it was a historic moment of justice: the return of the territory seized by force of arms at the end of the First Opium War ended China's humiliation at the hand of foreigners. The British position was a bit more complex. They not only regretted the loss of this economically valuable and prestigious enclave in the Far East, but felt that their stewardship, however attained, had brought prosperity and rule of law, in distinct contrast to the deadly political upheavals that had plagued the rest of China while Hong Kong developed into a modern and urbane centre of commerce and finance. In the middle were the people of Hong Kong themselves, many of whom had fled the Communist regime, only to find it once again on their doorsteps. They desired independence but Beijing would not hear of this, nor would the British government grant them the right of residence in the UK.

The handover was preceded by several years of negotiations between

Hong Kong's towers of finance, symbols of capitalism

Beijing and London. Although Hong Kong Island was ceded 'in perpetuity' to the British by an 1842 treaty, the mainland areas of Kowloon and the New Territories (without which the colony would have been untenable) had been acquired in 1898 on a 99-year lease which was due to expire. Deng Xiaoping proposed the concept of 'one country, two systems', which guaranteed Hong Kong the right to continue its capitalist economy and legal system for 50 years after the handover. Deng, however, was adamant about the return to full Chinese sovereignty, and films of his meeting with then British Prime Minister Margaret Thatcher are a study in cultural distance: Lady Thatcher attempted to smile politely while the diminutive Deng chain-smoked, gesticulated, and expectorated into a spittoon at his feet. After 22 rounds of negotiations, the Joint Declaration establishing the Hong Kong Special Administrative Region was signed.

The people of Hong Kong, fearing the worst, began to make plans to leave by acquiring foreign passports. After the June 1989 events on Tiananmen Square, apprehension turned into a palpable fear. Then, after Prince Charles and Chris Patten sailed away aboard the royal yacht *Britannia*, Hong Kong was hit by a

The Hong Kong Convention and Exhibition Centre holds many international events

series of problems unrelated to politics. The Southeast Asian economic crisis arrived within days after the handover, roiling the stock market, and a few years later the SARS epidemic not only took the lives of hundreds, but caused an evaporation of tourist revenue. In both cases, Beijing came to the rescue with massive input of capital.

Today, although Beijing appoints the Chief Executive, nominally Hong Kong's leader (much as London had appointed the Governor General), the fears of goose-stepping PLA soldiers and heavy-handed political commissars in Mao suits have largely disappeared. Personal and press freedoms are much the same as before the handover. Business is booming, as Hong Kong companies take advantage of China's increasing prosperity. Rather than Communist hard-liners, more concern today is given to the competitive capitalists of Shanghai.

Traditionally more of a dormitory zone for the business districts on Hong Kong Island, it has developed as an industrial (and now a shopping) centre in its own right.

Kowloon Park

This glorious green, shaded and ornamented park in the heart of downtown Kowloon has lakes, flower gardens, children's playgrounds, an outdoor art gallery called the Sculpture Walk and an indoor sports complex. The Kowloon Mosque stands in the southeast corner of the park.

22 Austin Road, between Nathan Road & Kowloon Park Drive.
Tel: (0852) 2724 3344.
Open: 6am–midnight. Free admission.
MTR station: Tsim Sha Tsui.

Museum of Art

The museum's six exhibition galleries contain a fine selection of historical and contemporary Chinese art, including lithographs of old Hong Kong. Visiting exhibitions from around the world vary the programme, but the emphasis is on Chinese antiquities, fine arts, historical Hong Kong and contemporary works by Hong Kong artists. One gallery contains the Xubaizhai collection of historical Chinese painting and calligraphy.

Cultural Centre, 10 Salisbury Road, Tsim Sha Tsui, adjacent to the Star Ferry Pier. Tel: (0852) 2734 2167.
Open: Mon–Wed, Fri & Sat 10am–6pm, Sun 1–6pm. Closed: Thurs.
Admission charge. MTR station: Tsim Sha Tsui.

Neon lights on Nathan Road in Kowloon

Hong Kong Island and harbour from Kowloon

Museum of History

This excellent museum traces 6,000 years of Hong Kong history, from the earliest traces of human habitation through the many dynasties of China, to the foundation of the British colony and Hong Kong's subsequent development to become one of the world's most fascinating cities. Highlights are the archaeological finds from Tang-Dynasty kilns, and Song- and Ming-Dynasty villages.
Kowloon Park, 100 Chatham Road, Tsim Sha Tsui. Tel: (0852) 2724 9042.
Open: Tue–Sat 10am–6pm, Sun 1–6pm.
Closed: Mon. Admission charge.
MTR station: Tsim Sha Tsui.

Sung Dynasty Village

Despite the somewhat tacky and Disneyesque rendition of Chinese life and culture during the Sung (or Song) Dynasty (AD 960–1279), this still

THE OPIUM WARS

China was forcibly opened to the world by the British in the aftermath of the Opium Wars of 1839–42 and 1856–60. Concerned that the profits of trade, in particular tea, were flowing too much in China's favour, Britain aimed to reverse this process by forcing opium grown in India on the Chinese. China protested against the 'foreign mud' that was turning its people into addicts, so Britain sent warships to protect the drug barons' interests. China fought back and lost.

South China was the initial flash-point of the conflict. After Emperor Qianlong's entreaties to Queen Victoria were ignored, he dispatched an official, Lin Zexiu, to stop the trade. Lin had 20,000 chests of British opium dumped in the harbour. Outraged by this act of 'piracy', the British warships opened fire.

While individual Chinese bear no ill will to foreigners for these acts – they've seen far worse under the Japanese and, some would say, indigenous overlords – the Chinese government never tires of mentioning this humiliating chapter in China's history, especially when lectured about human rights.

The Museum of Art in Hong Kong

succeeds in being fairly charming and interesting. Fortune-telling, martial arts displays, woodcarving, tea-making, marriage ceremonies and other traditional crafts and activities are represented by performers wearing traditional costume.
Kau Wah Keng, Lai Chi Kok. Open: 10am–8.30pm. Admission charge. MTR station: Mei Foo. Bus: 6A from the Kowloon Star Ferry Pier.

Waterfront Promenade

This colonnaded and traffic-free walkway, shaded from the sun, runs alongside Kowloon Public Pier, past the Clock Tower, the gracefully modern buildings of the Hong Kong Cultural Centre and the Space Theatre. It is a pleasant place to stroll at any time. It is also a popular place to sit and watch the busy harbour full of ships, from

junks to ocean-going tankers, as it offers an excellent vantage point for the glittering night-time view of Hong Kong Island across the water.
Adjacent to the Star Ferry Pier.

New Territories

The New Territories occupy a great swathe of mostly rugged territory between Kowloon and the Chinese border. Although parts are being filled in by fast-growing new towns, the New Territories retain much that is wild and natural, astonishingly so with Hong Kong so near.

Among the attractions in this area are Lau Fau Shan, a village on the northwest coast noted for its oysters (both their production and consumption); the Maclehose Trail, a long-distance footpath on the Tai Mo Hill; the Mai Po Marshes, a

notable spot for bird-watching on the northwest coast; and the Yuen Yuen Institute, a temple complex in which Buddhism, Taoism and Confucianism are represented, as well as a replica of Beijing's Temple of Heaven. If you lack your own transport, consider exploring the New Territories with one of the guided tours offered by the **HKTA** (Hong Kong Tourist Association).
HKTA. Toll-free tel: (800) 282 4582.
www.discoverhongkong.com

Macao

Formerly a Chinese territory under Portuguese administration, the settlement in Macao dates from 1557, although the right of permanent occupation was only granted to Portugal in 1887, and the territory returned to Chinese sovereignty in 1999. Today, 98 per cent of its population is Cantonese-speaking Chinese. The remainder is mostly Portuguese, with a sprinkling of other foreign nationals. A reclamation project has converted Taipa and Coloane islands into one island, making space for Macao's International Airport and increasing the territory's land area by 20 per cent.

Coloane Park

Covering 20 hectares (49 acres), the gardens are wonderfully colourful, with a wide range of trees, flowers and shrubs, as well as ponds and a walk-in aviary.
Coloane Island, near the Taipa-Coloane

causeway. Tel: (0853) 870 295. Open: 9am–7pm. Free admission. Bus: 21A.

Fortaleza da Guia (Guia Fort)

Dominating the highest point in Macao, this fort sits atop the green and tranquil Colina da Guia (Guia Hill). Among the old cannon-dotted walls, which date from the 1630s, are a lighthouse and a small church. The lighthouse dates from 1865 and is the oldest on the Chinese shoreline.

(continued on p118)

A traditional street shop

Tour: Hong Kong by public transport

This tour focuses on the heart of Hong Kong, around the harbour, and takes full advantage of the remarkable efficiency and frequency of services offered by its cheap public transport network, both on land and water.

Allow four hours to cover the 16-km (10-mile) tour.

Begin on Hong Kong Island at the Central Star Ferry Pier.

1 Star Ferry to Kowloon

The busy ferries, painted green and white, are a popular symbol of Hong Kong and are among the city's joys. They afford a ringside view of Victoria Harbour, one of the world's most fascinating and animated waterfront scenes, as well as of the serried ranks of skyscrapers on either shore.
Turn right from the Star Ferry Pier on the Kowloon side.

2 Kowloon Public Pier

A short circular detour on the elegantly modern peristyle walkway, beside the waterfront, leads past the venerable Clock Tower, the Hong Kong Cultural Centre and the Space Museum.
Walk down Nathan Road or turn on to Salisbury Road and take bus 1, 1A, 2, 6, 6A or 9. Get off at the Tsim Sha Tsui MTR station beside the mosque on Nathan Road.

3 Nathan Road

A little beyond the mosque is the entrance to Kowloon Park (*see p112*). Beyond the Park Lane Shoppers Boulevard lies a shoppers' paradise.
Walk northward along Nathan Road for about 500m (450yds) to the Jordan MTR station. Take the MTR to Central on Hong Kong Island. Turn right onto Des Voeux Road where the trams run. Continue for about 250m (275yds) and turn left up one of the small streets.

4 Mid-Levels Hillside Escalator

At 800m (2,625ft), the world's longest escalator ascends the steep hillside among shops, houses and restaurants. However, as the escalator goes only in one direction at a time (downwards 6am–10am, upwards 10.20am–midnight), it may be wise not to venture too far as you will have to return on foot.
Return to Des Voeux Road and take any eastbound tram. Get off in front of Chater Garden. Walk up Garden Road to the Peak Tram station.

5 Peak Tram

The tram glides uphill through rugged scenery to the finest view in Hong Kong, and to another good shopping centre.

Return on the Peak Tram and thence to Des Voeux Road Central. Then take any eastbound tram. Get off at Hong Kong Park.

6 Hong Kong Park

This provides a welcome break from the city, as well as being a place for early-morning tai chi exercises.

Go to the tram line on Queensway and take any eastbound tram. Get off at Pacific Place.

7 Pacific Place

The Pacific Place Shopping Mall is one of the principal venues for shopping, with many of the big names represented, and some excellent restaurants.

Return to Queensway and take any eastbound tram. Get off at the junction of Johnston Road and Hennessy Road. Either walk or take a taxi the short distance north to the Wan Chai Star Ferry Pier.

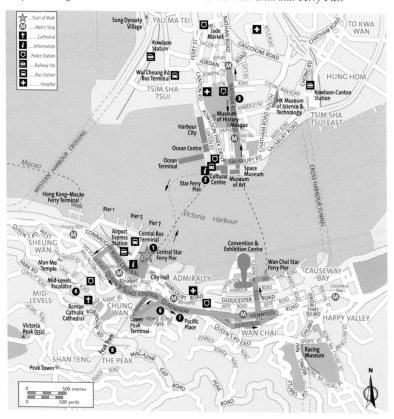

Tour: Hong Kong by public transport

Colina da Guia, above the Hong Kong-Macao ferry terminal. Tel: (0853) 569 808. Open: 9am–5.30pm. Free admission.

Fortaleza do Monte (Mount Fortress)

The powerful defensive Citadel of Macao was built between 1617 and 1626, and was responsible for the defeat of a Dutch invasion force in 1622. It now houses the Macao weather observatory, and offers fine views over the town.

Travessa dos Artilheiros, Macao town centre, adjacent to the Igreja de São Paulo (see listing below). Tel: (0853) 363 057. Open: 6am–7pm (May–Sept); 7am–6pm (Oct–Apr). Free admission.

Igreja de São Paulo (Church of St Paul)

The fine baroque façade and stairway are all that remain of this 17th-century Catholic church. Built between 1602 and 1637 with the help of Japanese Christians who had fled persecution in Nagasaki, it was all but destroyed by a fire in 1835.

Rua da Ressurreição, Macao town centre, adjacent to Mount Fortress. Free admission.

Fortaleza do Monte in Macao

Kum Iam Tong
(Kun Iam Tong Temple)

The 360-year-old Ming-dynasty
Buddhist temple is dedicated to the
Queen of Heaven and the Goddess of
Mercy. It is the largest temple in Macao,
and around one of its altars are three
gold-lacquered statues of the Buddha.
In the garden is the Lover's Tree, which,
according to legend, arose on the spot
where a suicide pact was observed by
two young lovers.
*Avenida do Coronel Mesquita, Macao
town centre. Tel: (0853) 556 127.
Open: 7am–6pm. Free admission.*

Leal Senado (Municipal Council)

The Loyal Senate House dates from
1784, and contains a stone tablet,
inscribed in Portuguese, describing
Macao as the 'City of the name of God,
Macao, there is none more loyal'
because it remained loyal to Portugal
when the home country was occupied
by the Habsburgs.

GAMBLING IN MACAO

A third of Macao's revenues come from
gambling, conducted in a constellation
of eight casinos operated under a
government franchise by a local business
syndicate, and recently a Las Vegas-based
company. Masses of slot machines can be
played alongside Western casino games
such as blackjack, baccarat and roulette,
as well as such popular Chinese ones as
fan tan, dai siu (big-small), *pai ko* and
keno. In addition, there is dog-racing
at the Canidrome and horse-racing at
the Macao Jockey Club's racetrack on
Taipa Island.

Sino-Portuguese shop-houses in Macao's
main square

*Largo do Senado, Macao town centre.
Tel: (0853) 387 333.
Open: Mon–Sat 1–7pm. Closed: Sun.
Free admission.*

Museu da Taipa
(Taipa House Museum)

A museum housed in one of the
old Portuguese colonial villas in
Taipa village, this is devoted to
exhibiting the old style of life in
the territory.
*Avenida da Praia, near the Taipa-
Coloane causeway. Tel: (0853) 825 314.
Open: 10am–6pm. Admission charge.
Bus: 21A from Macao.*

Getting away from it all

No country that occupies such a vast extent of the planet as China could be short of places renowned for natural beauty. This seems even more true because of the great emphasis Chinese poets and painters have always placed on their land's scenic wonders, as though beauty to delight the senses and inspire the mind was part of the contract between the Middle Kingdom and the Heaven that watched over it.

Hopefully the preceding chapters of this book have led the reader to some oases of tranquillity, even in the midst of huge cities. The parks of Shanghai and the Water Towns offer respite from urban stress and the fascinating but sometimes frenetic visits to historical sights. We cruised the majestic Yangzi River and climbed the sacred mountain of Emei Shan, which, if one has the time to explore, can be quite relaxing. This chapter takes us further afield, from the highlands of Tibet to an island with a distinctively religious atmosphere, not far from Shanghai, to two unique destinations in the southwest Yunnan Province.

Hutiao Xia (Tiger Leaping Gorge)

This 30-km (19-mile) section of the Yangzi River surges through a gorge which takes its name from a local legend that the gorge is so narrow that a tiger was able to escape pursuing hunters by leaping across it. From the top of the Yulong Xue Shan (Jade Dragon Snow Mountain) to the level of the river it is a dizzying 4,000m (13,120ft). At the village of Qiaotou at the upstream end of the gorge, one is basically at water level, but at the mid-point of the gorge, called Hutaoyuan (Walnut Grove), you are looking down 2,000m (6,560ft) to the turbulent river below, and looking across at a cliff so large that perceptions become oddly distorted. The best way to enjoy the gorge is to take a trek along the less precipitous north side, through charming villages and rice fields, and stay at friendly guesthouses along the way. Depending on your speed, it takes two or three days to reach Walnut Grove where a minibus can whisk you back to Qiaotou. Ponies with guides are also available for hire, to carry you or your bags, but check with locals as to current conditions since the undertaking becomes risky when the weather turns bad. If time or fitness doesn't allow, take a minibus to Walnut Grove and return to Qiaotou.

The pristine waters of the Yangzi flow through Yunnan Province

Avoid the heavily touristed rickshaw rides on the south side of the gorge. *Qiaotou village, 100km (65 miles) north of the town of Lijiang in Yunnan Province. Open: 8am–5pm. Admission charge.*

Putuoshan Dao (Putuoshan Island)

This small (8km/5 miles from top to bottom) island located in Huangda Bay east of Hangzhou is sacred to Buddhists and receives a large number of Chinese tourists attempting to rediscover their religious roots. Once home to over 2,000 monks, it was badly desecrated and depopulated during the Cultural Revolution, but tourist revenues are now paying to refurbish the temples.

While the temples are interesting – in particular the restored Fayu Si (Fayu Temple), which was moved here from Nanjing by order of the emperor in 1689 – the religious sights are not what would attract a visitor seeking peace and solitude, since, especially at weekends, they are filled with pilgrims. Rather it is recommended to seek out the tranquillity of the beaches, quiet pathways leading to isolated pavilions, and the caves which dot the island. On the east coast of the island, the Baibusha (One Hundred Step Beach) and just around the point the even calmer Qianbusha (One Thousand Step Beach) are quiet and relaxing, but the Houaisha (Hou'ai Beach) on the north shore guarantees solitude. Near the Fanyin Dong (Fanyin Cave) on the east side of the island there are spectacular views of the East China Sea far below. In the southeast of the island a 33-m-high (110-ft) statue of Guanyin, the Goddess of Mercy, is visited by thousands of pilgrims annually.

The island is accessible by boat from Shanghai (12 hours) or by a fast ferry from the town of Ningbo in Zhejiang Province. It's now a four-hour drive from Shanghai to Ningbo, crossing the newly opened Hangzhou Wan Daqiao (Hangzhou Bay Bridge). Accommodation is available in the village at the south end of the island near the ferry landing. Admission charge for the island.

Xizang (Tibet)

North from Qiaotou, you are surrounded by lovely hillsides covered with walnut and spruce trees with occasional stone farmhouses, but in an abrupt transition the trees turn to grasslands and the road straightens: you've just reached the geographical (although not political) edge of the

The Potala Palace in Tibet stands resilient and proud in spite of turmoil in the region

Tibetan Buddhist monks overlooking Ganden Monastery

Tibetan Plateau. Arid after spring and with patches of snow even in the summer, the white peaks of the Himalayas loom in the distance. With white *chorten* (the Tibetan word for pagoda) festooned with colourful prayer flags, and long-haired yak grazing amidst alpine wildflowers, the area lies in stark contrast to the lower parts of Yunnan.

The Qinghai–Tibet Plateau, with an average altitude of 4,000m (13,120ft), and the Himalayan mountains, rising to 8,848m (29,030ft) at the summit of Everest, are the defining physical characteristics of Tibet.

A distinctive Buddhist tradition, with the priest-ruler Dalai Lama at its head, and a society that, until recently, was rooted in the medieval world, are its defining social characteristics.

Unfortunately, Tibet's tranquil and ordered existence has been disrupted since 1951, when the once independent country was occupied by Chinese forces and subjected to a massive influx of ethnic Chinese. Periodic bouts of rebellion are ruthlessly suppressed. Despite this sombre political background, Tibet exercises an almost talismanic effect on foreign tourists, even allowing for the difficulties of getting there and the physical challenges involved in simply getting around on the 'roof of the world'.

It is possible to reach Tibet by both bus and train, but the most convenient way is to fly. Connections

The magnificent scenery of Shangri-La

can be made to Lhasa from all major airports in China. Trains from all over the country now connect with the new Golmud–Lhasa line, the highest railway in the world.

Lhasa

The capital city's altitude of 3,700m (12,140ft) above sea level can make it forbidden territory for those prone to suffering from altitude sickness. The old Tibetan quarter of the city is an atmospheric, if somewhat odiferous, warren of narrow streets and alleys where you may see people spinning prayer wheels as commonly as they talk or walk in the street.

The highlight of any visit is the stunning 17th-century Budala Gong (Potala Palace), formerly the seat of government and residence of the Dalai Lama, before which pilgrims prostrate themselves. Almost as impressive is the Dazhao Si (Jokhang Temple), Tibet's most important religious building, dating from the 7th century and containing a statue of the child Sakyamuni which the faithful believe was carved by the Buddha himself.

Outside the city, trips can be made to the Everest Base Camp at Rongbuk.

Zhongdian (Shangri-La)

The town of Zhongdian, about 200km (125 miles) north of Lijiang in Yunnan Province, is an old Tibetan trading town, now re-branded as Shangri-La by the Chinese tourist authorities based on a somewhat dubious claim that the best-selling 1933 novel, *Lost Horizon*, set in a paradisiacal Himalayan mountain valley, was based on the area. Zhongdian is hoping to become another Lijiang and the revived old town is amusing, with folk dances held in the central square which visitors are welcome to join, and restored Tibetan-style houses along cobblestone streets. As in Lijiang, the old town is adjoined by a modern Han Chinese city. It has an airport with direct flights to Beijing and Shanghai and lies at a base altitude of 3,000m (9,840ft).

About 4km (2½ miles) north of town, in the village of Songzhanling, lies **Ganden Sumtseling Gompa (Sumtseling Monastery)**, an important monastery of the Gelugpa (yellow hat) sect (*Open: 7am–4pm. Admission charge*). The central building of the complex bears a striking resemblance to the Potala Palace in Lhasa, and is tended by hundreds of monks, especially at festival times, making it the largest Tibetan lamasery in Yunnan. There are other local sights of interest, such as the Napa Hai wetlands, migration point of the black-necked crane.

From here it's an incredibly beautiful (although frankly not for the acrophobic) 180-km (110-mile) drive to Deqen. Give this one-street town a miss and continue a few kilometres to the temple and village of Feilaisi, which has guesthouses looking across the valley to the object of your trip, the majestic **Meili Xue Shan (Meili Snow Mountain)**, the highest peak in Yunnan at an altitude of 6,740m (22,100ft). Meili Snow Mountain has never been conquered, in spite of several attempts by serious mountaineers.

Rise with the sun and watch the colours caress the looming peaks of Meili as Tibetan prayer flags flutter behind the *chortens* of Feilaisi. The drive to Meili Snow Mountain first descends to the Mekong River, called the Lancang Jiang, meaning 'winding river', by the Chinese. A bridge crosses the river and leads to a base camp (which also has guesthouses) at the foot of the mountain. The mountain (*Open: 8am–5pm. Admission charge*) is sacred to Tibetans and there is a pilgrim's path both climbing and circumscribing it. It's best to climb aboard a pony for the 15-km (9½-mile) ascent through pine and spruce forests to the foot of the glacier. Here, you will surely conclude, is the reasonable end of your trip as you gaze upward at steep cliffs and clouds of swirling snow.

There are a number of daily flights to Shangri-La from Kunming, the provincial capital. Alternatively, buses from Lijiang leave at least 12 times a day and take 5 hours.

Sumtseling Monastery

When to go

Compared to the often frigid north of the country, the climate of the south will generally come as a relief. Summer is still hot, but winters are milder. Along the coastal regions, including Shanghai, humidity is the bane of the summer months. The frequent rains of that season provide momentary respite, although summer is also the typhoon season. As in the north, spring and autumn are glorious and the ideal time for a visit, when the climate is at its most temperate.

The word 'typhoon' is of Chinese origin and means 'great wind', so put your travel plans by air on hold when a typhoon is predicted, since the airlines prudently cancel flights. Away from the coast the humidity in summer is not a problem, but winters can be quite cold. Tibet is pleasantly cool in the summer but bitterly cold with snow in the winter. Also be prepared for winter snow at the high altitudes in the provinces of Yunnan and Sichuan.

Given the choice, take autumn – the air is cleaner after the rains of summer. One caveat here, however: the major national holidays, the first week of May and the first week of October, free the Chinese from their jobs and they take to the roads, rails and planes in vast numbers, making travel difficult.

Still, if you are safely ensconced in a pre-booked hotel, it's a fun time for enjoying the festivities and people-watching.

Shanghai grandparents love to tell the kids tales of the city blanketed in snow, but with increased urbanisation coupled with global warming, it's more likely to be rain that falls in Shanghai during the winter. The now widespread

WEATHER CONVERSION CHART

25.4mm = 1 inch
$°F = 1.8 × °C + 32$

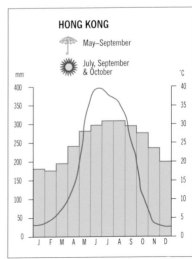

HONG KONG

May–September

July, September & October

The vast country offers a range of spectacular landscapes

use of air-conditioning in hotels, restaurants and shops makes the heat of summer more bearable, and mornings and early evenings are the best time for an outdoor stroll. Shanghai is located at 31 degrees northern latitude, and the climate can roughly be compared to that of the southern Mediterranean coast of Spain or the southeastern coast of the USA.

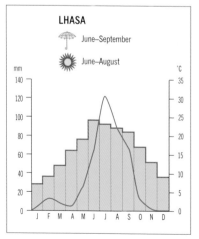

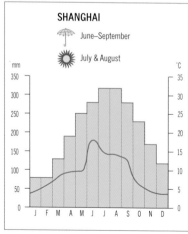

Getting around

Transportation systems and the infrastructure which support them have improved greatly during the past few years, which is merciful, given the long distances that need to be covered. Gone are the days of white-knuckle experiences in ageing Russian aircraft plying domestic routes, and improved roads mean that travelling times by car or bus have been cut by half. Shanghai has an excellent and ever-expanding underground and light rail mass transit system, as do Hong Kong and Guangzhou.

Still, given the vast distances and sometimes forbidding terrain, coupled with the increased demand on all public travel systems by the newly mobile local population, all travel options can at times be a challenge to the visitor. Foreigners on organised tours should have few complaints about transport, although some tours and visits are liable to cancellation at short (or zero) notice for reasons which are not always explained. Independent travellers' main problem will be the language barrier.

By air

Air China (*www.air-china.com*), the Chinese national carrier, has an excellent reputation for safety and efficiency. State-of-the-art equipment and well-trained staff have led seasoned international travellers to compare it favourably to Western airlines. Air China operates domestic flights as well, as do a plethora of smaller Chinese airlines, notably the Shanghai-based **China Eastern Airlines** (*www.ce-air.com*). Shanghai's futuristic **Pudong Airport** (*Tel: (021) 9608 1388. www.shanghaiairport.com/en*) is shockingly efficient, and connected to the city by the world's first magnetic levitation (mag-lev) train. Many domestic flights use the older **Hongqiao Airport** (*Tel: (021) 5260 4620. www.shanghaiairport.com/en*), which has flights to any city in China with an airport. Domestic air travel in China is not expensive by international standards – there are even some privately owned budget carriers. Booking as far in advance as possible

THOMAS COOK'S CHINA

'The first real railway line in China was opened last September with unexpected éclat, between Tientsin [Tianjin], Taku and Tongshan. The length of the line is only eighty-six and a half miles [138km], but the success achieved is a great factor towards future development in this direction [...]'.

From Cook's *Excursionist and Tourist Advertiser*, 14 December 1888.

will improve your chances of getting the best price.

By train

Railways are China's arteries, the most economical, safe and reliable way of travelling long distances, thus the choice of the Chinese themselves. Without them the country would suffer some kind of fatal seizure, although sometimes trying to get on a train might do the same for foreign travellers. It is important to have sharp elbows, a note in Chinese stating the ticket type desired, and a willingness to kowtow to the ticket clerk, who will pronounce with the finality of an emperor on one's travel plans. Alternatively, have your hotel concierge or a reliable travel agent handle this for you. Avoid the touts selling tickets around the train stations.

Once you find the right platform in an overcrowded station, the rest should go smoothly. Riding soft class, or soft class sleeper, is a good way to travel in China: a closed door compartment contains four bunks and you're provided with clean linen, curtains, and meals in a dining car. Hard class is something else – particularly a hard seat on a long-distance train, though a hard sleeper can also be, well, hard, with six bunks in an open compartment, stacked three high.

Virtually the entire country is connected to the rail network, including a recently opened line to Lhasa, the capital of Tibet. Modern

Pudong International Airport, Shanghai, is an example of China's big leap into the modern era

express trains ply the 1,500 km (930 miles) from Shanghai to Beijing in 12 hours of climate-controlled luxury. A trip from Shanghai to Nanjing takes three hours on another modern express route, complete with double-deck carriages.

Chengdu North Train Station. Bei Erhuan.
Chongqing Train Station. Zaozi Gangya Zhen.
Guangzhou Train Station. Huanshi Xi.
Hong Kong Hung Hom and KCR East Rail Terminal. Cheong Wan Road, Kowloon.
Shanghai Train Station ticket office. 230 Beijing Dong & 1738 Beijing Xi.
Open: 8am–6pm.

Trams still operate on Hong Kong Island

By other public transport

Visitors to Shanghai will no doubt want to try the city's urban rapid transit system known as the MRT (or *ditie* in Chinese). Especially given the sometimes gridlocked streets above ground, it is often the quickest way to get anywhere within the city, including Pudong and the outlying suburbs. There are currently seven lines in operation (out of a planned 18), including north–south, east–west, and circular routes. The major interchange of the system is People's Square. The basic fare is a mere 3RMB, and stored-value tickets whisk you through the turnstiles. Announcements and station signage are in both English and Chinese.

The less agreeable aspect is the pushing of passengers entering and exiting the carriages, especially at crowded peak times.

Bus travel within a city is only useful if you truly know your route, since announcements and signage are in Chinese only. Long-distance buses are most useful to reach destinations not on the railway network. The advantages over trains is that the departures are more frequent and bus stations easier to reach than train stations. There are at least four in Shanghai and other large cities, one for each of the cardinal points of the compass, so that if your destination is north, for example, you'll look for the Northern Bus Station. Buses generally take less time than trains, especially on the many new improved roads across China. However, this convenience is purchased at the cost of comfort and safety. Driving standards are abysmal and accidents not uncommon. Even when you arrive safely, you'll often be shattered by recollections of the driver's use of the horn rather than the brakes. Long-distance buses also entertain their passengers with high-volume kung fu movies, which might not be to your taste.

Shanghai Bus Station. 666 Tianyaoqiao. Tel: (021) 6426 5558.
Hengfeng Road Bus Station.
270 Hengfeng. Tel: (021) 6317 3912.
Long-distance Bus Station, Hutai.

Tel: (021) 5661 8801.
Xujiahui Bus Station, Hongqiao.
Tel: (021) 6469 7325.

By taxi and car hire

Taxis abound in Shanghai and all other Chinese cities. Rates are not expensive and the meter should always be used: if the driver doesn't want to use the meter, get out of the taxi. No tipping is expected, and most drivers speak little or no English. Have your destination written in Chinese or show the driver a map with Chinese characters. Private car hire in China always includes a driver, since only foreigners with residence visas can obtain the requisite Chinese driver's licence.

Taxis in Shanghai are easily identified

Accommodation

Hotels in China present the full range of standards. Joint ventures with some of the world's leading hotel groups have led to the development of hotels in the major tourist and international business zones whose commitment to quality is impeccable. As the Chinese take to the road, the supply of mid-range hotel options is increasing, in turn decreasing prices and improving quality. Budget options are also available, and can sometimes be surprisingly agreeable, sometimes a decision to regret.

International chains such as Hyatt, Shangri-La, Mandarin and St Regis have all established flagship properties of an extremely high standard, with prices to match. Luxurious spas, in-room Jacuzzi tubs, private butlers, décor by internationally renowned designers, and *haute cuisine* are all available for those wishing to open their wallets. Just beneath such lofty citadels of the good life lies the domain of the locally managed high-end hotels, which still offer all the services and standards that one would find at home, but without the polished service of the international chains. In the mid-range you'll find a perfectly acceptable place to spend a few nights, but nothing approaching luxury, variable service, absent foreign language skills, and the occasional unpleasant surprise of noisy neighbours and leaky faucets.

There are now even chains of lower mid-range to budget hotels with perfectly acceptable accommodations (without restaurant facilities), such as the Home Inn or Motel 168 chains. Remember, however, that these chains target Chinese travellers, so get ready with your phrase book, and expect to be in a less-than-central location.

As supply increases, advance reservations are becoming less of a necessity except at peak periods such as Spring Festival in late January, and the two great Chinese holiday breaks, the first weeks of May and October, when not only are hotels (except the top tier) fully booked, but legally permitted by the government to increase their rates by 50 per cent.

Of course, it is reassuring to have a room booked when arriving in a strange city abroad. Plenty of internet-based travel agencies offer this service, sometimes with comments from previous guests. Check the location of the hotel carefully: Chinese cities are always surrounded by large suburbs, far from the attractions you've come to see.

If you arrive without a reservation, take no notice of the posted rates – discounts are almost always available, ranging from 30 to 50 per cent. At mid-range (and below) hotels, it's a good idea to see the room before registering. You will be asked to show your passport and pay a deposit – often for the full amount of your stay – plus a security deposit. Be sure to keep your receipt. Not all hotels of the mid-range and below categories will accept credit cards, so be sure to enquire in advance. Check-out time is invariably 12 noon, and half-day rates are charged if you wish to stay even a few hours longer. Internet facilities are available in all hotels of mid-range and above. Most rooms in China will be supplied with tea sachets, bottled water and a kettle. Tap water is not generally safe for drinking. Mid-range hotels will also have a mini-bar with soft drinks and beer.

Hotel fires occur too frequently in China. Smoke alarms are not common, but heavy drinking and smoking are. Check for fire exits on your floor. Single male guests will often receive telephone calls proposing 'massages': those foolish enough to accept this solicitation could find themselves victims of robbery or worse. If you receive such a call, unplug your telephone until morning, or telephone the reception telling them to block calls to your room. Theft by hotel staff is extremely rare in China, but take common-sense precautions, such as putting any valuables in a locked suitcase, or if the hotel has an in-room safe, use it.

It must be said that while standards of cleanliness and efficiency are improving, Chinese hotels are generally modern and without character. Some small inns are to be found in Shanghai's former French Concession, and a few colonial buildings in Guangzhou and Xiamen have been converted into hotels, but those seeking accommodation in traditional-style Chinese buildings will need to look long and hard. In small towns and villages, homestays are starting to blossom. While the experience will no doubt be interesting, expect to live like the locals. Camping is possible, but only as part of an organised tour specialising in these activities. It is usually possible to stay at pilgrims' inns at religious sites such as

Shanghai's Peace Hotel

The Shangri-La Hotel on Pudong

the sacred Taoist or Buddhist mountains, but again, prepare for the Spartan experience.

Star ratings

The government-mandated star rating system is a good, but not absolutely uniform, guide. Stars are awarded mostly on service quality, facilities and hygiene, but political connections can influence allocation. Ratings of 1 to 3 stars are awarded by provincial authorities, with 3 stars having to be approved by the national tourism administration. Ratings of 4 and 5 stars can only be awarded by the national authority. Be especially careful at the 5-star level: this is where local connections can come into play. With few exceptions, only the international chains have facilities that qualify them to be considered true 5-star hotels.

No stars: while much depends on the attitude of staff, the quality in such establishments is usually disappointing. Sometimes the proprietors know this from past experience with foreign guests and you will be told that the hotel is full even if it is not.

1-star: simple, but with air-conditioning, sometimes a coffee shop and a majority of rooms with private bath (below 250RMB).

2-star: air-conditioned, most rooms with private bath, offering Chinese food (250–830RMB).

3-star: fully decorated and well-equipped rooms, lifts, IDD telephones in rooms, television, in-house movies, 24-hour running hot and cold water (830–1,250RMB).

4-star: deluxe, fully equipped rooms, with extras such as hairdryers, business centre, fitness centre, swimming pool, medical centre and a range of restaurants and bars (1,250–3,000RMB).

5-star: standards which match the very best in the world (3,000RMB and above).

Hotel Sofitel, Shanghai

Food and drink

The Chinese love to eat not only for sustenance and taste but for the social aspect of communal dining. Dishes are placed on a revolving platform in the middle of the table and shared by all and you will be served an individual bowl of rice upon which to place the pieces you take from the communal serving plates. A common greeting, 'Chi fan le mei you?' literally means 'Have you eaten yet?'

Shanghai offers the most wide-ranging and eclectic culinary experience in China. All of the regional cuisines of China, from delicate Cantonese to spicy Sichuan, are here, as well as other Asian cuisines, notably Thai, Indian and Japanese. Those hungry for a taste of home need not worry: European restaurants are also popular with the locals.

While not all Chinese are gourmets, it is rare to find one that does not enjoy food. They can do so with a clear conscience and on the very best of authorities: Confucius himself pointed out that 'eating is the first happiness'. Chinese dining

Chinese soup

etiquette is rather unrestrained, with slurping of soup definitely permitted and bones left on the table. Tipping is uncommon in Chinese restaurants, although in expensive restaurants a service charge may be added to the bill.

Cuisines
Shanghai
Being close to the ocean, as well as major lakes and rivers, the cuisine of Shanghai relies heavily on fish and crustaceans. Freshness is of the essence, thus many Shanghainese favourites are available only during their brief season. A prime example of this is hairy crab (*da zha*), which is available only in the autumn. These are fresh-water crabs from the Yangzi and nearby lakes, which are lightly steamed and served with a variety of dips. Crystal prawns (*xia ren*) are marinated in egg white and brine and stir-fried. Many fish dishes are 'red cooked', meaning stir-fried in soy sauce and sugar. Truthfully, Shanghai's cuisine is not one of the most famous of

Chinese regional cuisines and is fairly described as 'comfort food' rather than *haute cuisine*. Although the proud locals would not admit this, the popularity of restaurants serving Cantonese and other regional cuisines, as well as Western and Japanese restaurants, in Shanghai seems to suggest otherwise.

Cantonese

Guangdong Province, the source of Cantonese cuisine, is an extremely fertile area yielding several harvests annually, and with a long coastline that provides an abundance of seafood. These fresh ingredients are mostly steamed or stir-fried, ensuring that their flavour and texture are retained. As a result they need little support in the way of spices or sauces, although light sauces of garlic, ginger and spring onions are favoured.

Sichuan

Spice is the variety of life in Sichuan, and the fiery taste of the province's cuisine, laced with red-hot peppers,

Kiosk selling hot chestnuts on the Bund, Shanghai

CHOPSTICKS

Chopsticks can be awkward at first. Perseverance is needed to get the technique right, but a Chinese meal is best enjoyed with them, and the two sticks can be surprisingly agile in practised hands. The bottom stick is the 'anvil', held firmly between the first joint of the ring finger and the lower thumb, while resting in the crook of forefinger and thumb. The top stick is held like a pen between the tip of the thumb and forefinger, and pivots against the lower stick. Practice makes perfect!

---

is renowned throughout China. The pepper varieties in Sichuan give food a sharp, lemony taste, which is different from the standard chilli flavour. Although hot and spicy is the basic approach, the cuisine offers much more, and chefs work with a medley of seven tastes – sweet, sour, salty, fragrant, bitter, nutty and hot – to get the balanced effect they are seeking. Sichuan's subtlety is present in tea-smoked and camphor-smoked duck, while tangerine-peel chicken, pork with vegetables and bamboo shoots in a sweet sauce are delicately flavoured dishes.

Crabs are a speciality in Canton

Since all regional cuisines are available in Shanghai and other cities of southern China, it is worth noting them here:

Beijing

The signature dish of the capital, Beijing duck, is served throughout China. Famous restaurants specialise in serving only this dish. The recipe requires a special type of duck, an elaborate method of preparation, and cooking in a special type of oven, all necessary to assure that the skin is both crispy and succulent. The skin and meat of the roasted duck are cut thinly and eaten in pancakes along with spring onions, cucumber and sweet plum sauce. The meal ends with a soup made from the duck's carcass.

Vegetarian

Despite the range of options available, vegetarians may be a bit hard put to find suitable eating choices. Vegetarianism in China is practised for spiritual not health reasons. The best bet for finding vegetarian fare is around Buddhist temples.

Other

In Muslim restaurants and households, particularly in the far west, mutton takes the place of pork and pilaf rice is used in place of plain boiled. Hunan likes its spices but uses them in a more restrained way than Sichuan. Few dishes enjoy the exotic reputation of the Mongolian hotpot, which helps the northerners survive their long

CHINA AND TEA

Lu Yu, a Tang-Dynasty Master of Tea, wrote that drinking tea aids the digestion, especially 'when sipped in the company of sweet and beautiful maidens in a pavilion by a water-lily pond or near a lacquered bridge'. Most tea drinkers will not be so fortunate, but as long as the tea is good, they may be willing to make allowances. Suzhou is renowned for its teahouses. Fujian Province is home to China's best oolong teas and the famous Dragon Well green tea is grown near Hangzhou.

In the Chinese tea ceremony, the miniature cups and teapot are doused with scalding hot water. Tea is then placed in the pot, and boiling water added. After a brief infusion, the pot is emptied into the cups and the infusing process repeated.

There are many varieties of Chinese tea, and though jasmine tea is usually served as a matter of course in restaurants, you could ask for black, green, oolong or herbal tea instead.

and harsh winters, and is in fact a kind of soup in which vegetables and meat are first cooked in boiling water at the table, and then eaten. The bouillon gradually becomes more flavourful, and is drunk at the meal's end.

Beverages

Tea is the most popular drink in China (*see box opposite*), but other beverages, some far less benign, are indulged in. Sweet wines and liqueurs made from fruits, flowers or herbs can be tempting and sometimes potent drinks. Western-style wines are now produced in several regions of China. In Shanghai, brands such as Great Wall and Dynasty are well known, and while not world class, are quite drinkable. Beware of *mao tai* as it is extremely strong. It's the most famous of Chinese clear liquors and is used again and again in the *gan bei* ('bottoms up') toasts made at banquets. Chinese beer, especially the light and fragrant lager-style Tsingtao (which is still brewed according to a 1900s German recipe), is of a high standard and is extremely refreshing with spicy foods.

Food and drink

A Chinese tea ceremony

Entertainment

Shanghai is undoubtedly the entertainment capital of China. All tastes are catered to here: traditional Chinese opera, Western classical music performances and ballet, the country's best acrobatic circus, chic clubs, low dives, and even quiet pubs all abound in Shanghai. Not only local artists perform. Shanghai is the first stop for visiting performers from abroad. Outside of Shanghai and Guangzhou, the options are limited, especially if you're not fond of karaoke.

While Shanghai is best known as the most culturally avant-garde city in China, it still offers plenty for those seeking more classical and less raucous forms of entertainment. The Shanghai acrobatics troupe is world-renowned, and the local version of Chinese opera, called *kunju*, is just as interesting as the better-known Beijing version.

The best source of information on both upcoming performances and the hippest new nightspots are the English-language entertainment magazines *City Weekend* or *That's Shanghai*. These are distributed free in hotels and restaurants, and both have websites: *www.cityweekend.com.cn* and *www.thatssh.com*. *City Weekend* also publishes a Guangzhou edition. In Hong Kong look for *BC Magazine* or visit their website, *www.hk.bcmagazine.net*

Bars and pubs

If you feel like an evening drink without loud music or dancing,

Shanghai can oblige. The busiest watering holes are found cheek by jowl with the clubs of Maoming Road and are only differentiated by the lack of loud music. Mainly active on weekends, they cater mostly to Chinese and a few expats. The bars of Xintiandi are a bit less wild, but visitors are most likely to find something to their liking in the former French Concession, or in the larger international hotels. Theme bars are becoming popular, with everything from American Wild West saloons to British pubs competing for the drinker's time and money.

Cafés and teahouses

If it's not intoxication you seek, the cafés and teahouses of Shanghai are your best choice for people-watching and whiling away the day or evening hours. Suzhou and Hangzhou are famous throughout China for their traditional Chinese teahouses. They range from simple places frequented

Western-style cinema has a popular following

Nightclubs jostle with late-night shops in Hong Kong's Wanchai district

by elderly gentlemen to elegantly appointed pavilions alongside canals and lakes. The Starbucks chain has hit China full force, but there are many locally owned cafés that offer more for less. Light food is served in most cafés, although usually not in teahouses. The best place to have a tea or coffee in Shanghai is in a pavement café in the former French Concession.

Cinema

Shanghai was the Hollywood of China in the 1930s, but the Communists ended that rather quickly. Since the government bans or censors both foreign and (particularly) Chinese films, the fare in most cinemas is limited. Most people easily circumvent this by buying pirated DVDs which are available for a pittance, or downloading them from the internet. There are some art cinemas showing avant-garde films, usually near Shanghai's Moganshan Road art galleries. Again, check the entertainment magazines for current listings. Outside of Shanghai, if you want to relax over a movie, you'd best do it in your hotel room, which is likely to be equipped with a DVD player.

Clubs

Rock, jazz and hip-hop venues abound in Shanghai, some of them quite good, some atrocious. Jazz, being instrumental, speaks the universal language of melody and there are some good jazz clubs in town, usually more sedate than the rock-oriented venues. Maoming Road and the more upmarket Xintiandi area are the main music areas, but check the entertainment magazines for the current acts performing

Stylish dance clubs are favoured by the well-off young Shanghainese and expatriates. The latest mixes played by DJs who know the craft, English menus and attentive staff characterise these clubs. Cover charges can exceed 100RMB to keep out the proletariat, but single men should be warned that some of the sweet young ladies smiling across the bar may well be practitioners of the world's oldest profession.

Performing arts

Chinese acrobats, like their gymnasts, enjoy world-wide acclaim. High-wire balancing acts, plate-spinning, human pyramids and the like need no translation and make for an amusing evening fit for the whole family. Shanghai is traditionally the most famous venue for acrobatic performances.

A visit to a Chinese opera (*see feature pp34–5*) is an experience you won't forget. Yes, it's cacophonous, and no, you won't understand the dialogue, but most people come away with the feeling of having experienced something unique and extraordinary. There are now some venues that offer shortened versions and programmes in English, but they are obviously not the real thing. If you have the time and interest, try to seek out a traditional performance.

Classical music performances, both Western and Chinese, are another option for those seeking higher culture in their entertainment. Shanghai is justifiably proud of its Symphony Orchestra, and foreign orchestras often perform in the capital. The usual venue for such performances is the stunning Shanghai Grand Theatre.

Shopping

China manages to combine a great variety of styles, price ranges and standards in its shopping. By itself this is not so unusual, but the sheer range of shops, stalls and markets that it takes to serve its vast population is awesome. Visitors and locals are likely to have different interests in what they are looking to buy, but markets are definitely one of the best places to see the real China.

The Chinese are great shoppers and greater bargainers, so the energy is flowing. More importantly, the participants are focused on their shopping, not looking at you, so it's much easier to feel like the observer rather than the observed. If you want to join the game, it's essential, unless you visit only modern shopping malls, to be prepared to bargain. This doesn't come easily to most Westerners, but can be learned, and in fact is half the fun of shopping.

A few tips... If you're in a big market, such as Shanghai's Yu Yuan Bazaar, you'll quickly notice that many of the shops are selling identical items. Ask the price of your object of desire at a few, to get a rough idea of the asking price. You'll often get the price shown to you on a calculator, which is then handed to you to make a counter-offer. Start with 25 per cent of the asking price, which will probably be refused, so just smile and leave, but don't be surprised if you're called back. Above all, keep smiling.

While Shanghai and Hong Kong are certainly the best places for shopping in southern China, Suzhou and other cities have interesting markets. Almost every city has a *hua niao shichang* (bird and flower market) where local crafts are also sold. In Shanghai, besides Yu Yuan Bazaar, another popular shopping area for visitors is the Dongtai Road Antiques Market in the Luwan District.

For those not interested in the hustle and bustle of the market, the upscale malls of East Nanjing Road and the Bund are worth visiting. Here you'll find both Western luxury goods and dozens of smaller boutiques selling

COLLECTIONS

For those interested in seeing the original, unpurchasable treasures of China, the Shanghai Museum in People's Square and the Beijing Art Museum both have rare and exquisite exhibits. The Tsui Museum of Art in Hong Kong has a comprehensive collection that covers 5,000 years.

locally produced clothing as well as souvenirs. While much of the world's clothing is now produced in China, including top brands of sportswear, the real thing is no cheaper here than at home, so buy only what you might need for your trip.

Counterfeiting is big business in China. 'Designer clothes', 'antiques' and 'antiquities' are mass-produced in supposedly illegal factories (the Chinese authorities have done little to stamp them out). Remember that counterfeit goods, be they DVDs or clothing, are likely to be seized by customs authorities when you return home, and you could be subject to a fine as well.

Antiques – items not more than 180 years old, stamped with an official wax seal – should be what they purport to be: those from street markets are extremely unlikely to be genuine. Anything more than 180 years old is classed as an antiquity and cannot be exported, although occasionally you will be approached by people offering them. Don't even think about it. Another potential problem is the 'art student' scam, where a smiling young Chinese will suggest you go together to see great bargains at a special gallery he knows. Smile and depart. Despite all these caveats, there are plenty of fine products and souvenirs that one can bring back from China, so even confirmed non-shoppers should take enough time to consider the possibilities.

Colourful banners brighten the Yu Yuan Bazaar in Shanghai

Sport and leisure

Hiking and cycling opportunities abound outside the major urban centres. Specialised tour operators offer both trekking and cycling tours throughout the region, although Yunnan Province is considered the best place for these activities. Simply forgoing the cable cars and climbing the well-laid pilgrim paths and staircases on any of the sacred mountains is certainly good exercise. Along the coast, swimming and sailing are possible and Hainan Island is famous for its beaches.

The Chinese have their own sporting traditions, largely in the martial arts and softer permutations of it. *Wushu*, more commonly known as kung fu in the West, belongs to a tradition stretching back for thousands of years. Chinese wrestling, tai chi (*see box opposite*) and *qigong* (a fitness exercise aimed at controlling the mind and regulating breathing to improve overall health and physiology) are other examples of traditional Chinese sport. Courses in English can be arranged by fitness centres in hotels.

Participatory sports

Within the major cities of southern China, those seeking exercise are best advised to use the fitness centre of their hotel due to the air pollution. All of the top hotels in Shanghai and other major cities in southern China have fitness centres, a swimming pool and tennis courts. Some have evolved into spas and offer massage and other therapeutic treatments. Non-residents can often use the facilities by paying an entrance fee or by becoming a member of the hotel's club.

Golf in China is an extension of the board-room where deals are sealed between shots. There are over 20 courses in the countryside

Mah jong is a favourite pastime all over China

TAI CHI

Called *taijiquan* in Chinese, this is better known as tai chi in the West. It consists of a set of movements designed to exercise the body and mind. The aim is for the mind to control the movements of the body, which are graceful and gentle but complex. Many Chinese begin their day with a tai chi session in a park or in the street, and there is a restful, almost mesmerising, quality to the sight of hundreds of people moving to the natural rhythm of this exercise, which was formalised in the 17th century. People all over the world practise tai chi today, and if you have even a modicum of skill, you're welcome to join any group practising in China.

surrounding Shanghai and more around Guangzhou (*www.golfworldmap.com* & *www.golftoday.co.uk*). Bowling is a well-loved indoor sport, with hundreds of bowling alleys from deluxe to run-down found in all major cities (*www.cityweekend.com.cn*). Kite flying is a fun and relaxing way to spend an afternoon, too, and is engaged in on People's Square in Shanghai or any big public square throughout China.

Spectator sports

The 2008 Olympics increased China's passion for spectator sports and regular competitions are held. You can watch the Shanghai Sharks basketball team, where Yao Ming of NBA fame got his start, in action at Luwan Stadium from November to April. Formula One auto racing and Grand Prix motorcycle racing are held at the Shanghai International Circuit. The Shanghai Open Tennis tournament takes place in September. Check the entertainment magazines for details.

Early morning exercise, Shamian Island, Guangzhou

Children

China is not the easiest place to travel with children. The long travel times, the lack of attractions directed towards children, and the unfamiliarity of the food can make this a challenge for families. There are some specialist travel agencies which organise escorted tours especially for families with children that emphasise natural rather than cultural attractions, so if you're determined to show China to your children, this is your best choice.

Shanghai is certainly an easier place for families with young children than elsewhere in China, and the further one gets off the beaten track the more challenging it becomes. All the baby formula, disposable nappies and other assorted baby paraphernalia of the West are found in Shanghai and major cities.

In Shanghai, the **Shanghai Kejiguan (Science and Technology Museum)** is excellent (*2000 Zhongyang. Tel: (021) 6862 2000. Open: 9am–5pm. Admission charge. Metro: Shanghai Kejiguan*), and kite flying at **Renmin Gongyuan (People's Park)** is a good option when the weather is right (*Open: 6am–6pm. Admission charge. Metro: Renmin Gongyuan*). In fact throughout China, the central squares formerly used for mass political rallies have become kite-flying territory. **Aquaria 21** (*Gate 4, Chang Feng Gongyuan, 451 Da Du He. Tel: (021) 5281 8888. Open: 9am–5pm. Admission charge. Metro: Zhongshan Gongyuan then taxi*) in Chongning District is an excellent marine-themed attraction. The **Shanghai Zoo** (*Hongqiao Road, near Shanghai Airport. Tel: (021) 6268 7775. Open: 7am–5pm. Closed: Tue. Admission charge. Bus: 328, 911*) is a pleasant exception to the usual Chinese zoos with their bars and cages, which are usually depressing for adults and frightening for children who have

ONE-CHILD FAMILIES

Faced with the need to slow down the growth in China's population, the government adopted a 'one child per family' policy (national minorities are exempt). Large families are traditionally seen as a source of security for parents' old age, so the policy meant a traumatic change in lifestyle. Boys are preferred, and through ultrasound tests followed by abortion of female foetuses, the male/female ratio has been upset, with ten boys for every eight girls born. Ironically, China is also worried that pampered single children, or 'little emperors' as they are called, are growing up as a spoilt generation. Spoilt they may be, but in urban areas they are also stressed, as the family's expectations are channelled into the single child who studies hours unheard of in the West.

Having fun in the sea at Gulang Yu Island, Xiamen

been brought up with any conception of animal rights. A **Disneyland** (*Penny's Bay, Lantau Island. Tel: (852) 183 0830. Open: 10am–9pm (Apr–Oct); 10am–7pm (Nov–Mar). Admission charge. MTR: Sunny Bay*) operates in Hong Kong.

Children under 1.1m (3ft 4in) get half price at all attractions charging an entrance fee, but that's about the only accommodation made for the little ones. Restaurants rarely have high chairs suitable for young children and if you're travelling with a pushchair, you'll quickly notice that the pavements are irregular and escalators only run up.

The Chinese are quite demonstrative about their affection for children, including those of strangers. A blonde-haired blue-eyed toddler can be the source of so much attention as to make children (and their parents) a bit uncomfortable. It's not unheard of to have your child scooped up and hugged by complete strangers, and requests for photo opportunities can seem to never cease. Although the intention is good, it can become tiresome. On the other hand, the Chinese are likely to make a special effort to please families with children in hotels and restaurants.

Essentials

Arriving and departing

By air

Shanghai is proud of its futuristic Pudong Airport (*www.shanghaiairport.com/en*), connected to the city (not the centre, though) by the world's first magnetic levitation train. For domestic flights, however, you're more likely to use the older Hongqiao Airport (*www.shanghaiairport.com/en*). Hong Kong International Airport (*www.hongkongairport.com*) is connected to the city by the MTR rapid transit system. Airport taxes are included in the price of air tickets when they are purchased.

By road

It is possible to enter China by bus or on foot from Kazakhstan, Kyrgyzstan, Laos, Mongolia, Nepal, Pakistan, Russia and Vietnam.

By rail

From the south the only connection into China is on the Hong Kong–Guangzhou Express (*www.kcrc.com/html/eng*). From the north, more exotic routes, such as the Trans-Siberian Express (*www.trans-siberian.co.uk*) across Russia or Mongolia to Beijing, are also popular.

Customs regulations

The duty-free limits are 2 litres of alcohol, 600 cigarettes and 0.5 litres of perfume. There is a notional limit of 1,000 minutes of video film and 72 rolls of still film. Unlimited amounts of foreign currency can be imported, but amounts above US$10,000 need to have been declared and foreign exchange receipts retained if the balance is to be re-exported at the end of your trip. Chinese customs are tough with illegal narcotics and pornographic or anti-government literature. Excessive amounts of religious literature are also grounds for suspicion.

Electricity

The electricity supply is 220V, 50Hz AC. Several socket types are in use, for which a multiple adaptor plug should be purchased before departure.

Internet

While most hotels have Internet facilities, private Internet cafés are usually grim dens filled with chain-smoking teenagers playing online games. Wi-fi is common in Shanghai's hipper cafés.

Money

The main unit of currency is the *yuan* (¥) or *renminbi* (RMB). The *yuan* is divided into 10 *jiao*, and a *jiao* is divided into 10 *fen*. Notes come in denominations of 100, 50, 10, 5, 2 and 1 *yuan*, and 5, 2 and 1 *jiao*. Coins are 1 *yuan*, and 5, 2 and 1 *jiao*. Hong Kong and Macao have dollars and *pataca*, respectively. The HK Dollar (HK$) is divided into 100 cents. Notes come in denominations of HK$1000, 500, 100, 50, 10. Coins are HK$10 and 50, 20, 10, 5, 2, and 1 cent. The *pataca* (MOP$) is divided into 100 *avos*. Notes come in denominations of MOP$ 1000, 500, 100, 50, 10. Coins are 10, 5, 2, 1 *avos*.

Credit cards and ATMs

Credit cards are accepted in good restaurants, hotels and large tourist outlets. US dollars, euros and British pounds can be changed in banks and hotels. Exchange rates are centrally fixed, and there is no black market for currency. The easiest way to get Chinese cash is by using your credit card in a local ATM. Bank of China ATMs always accept foreign credit cards. Debit cards are less reliable, and bank-issued credit cards usually don't work.

Opening hours

Government offices and public institutions open Mon–Sat 8 or 9am–5 or 6pm, with a two-hour break at lunch, although some banks and foreign exchange offices may open on Sunday morning. Big department stores open daily 9am–7pm. Private businesses, such as shops and restaurants, open early and close very late.

Passports and visas

All visitors must obtain a visa before arrival from Chinese embassies and consulates, or at short notice from travel agencies in Hong Kong and Macao. Three-month and multiple-entry visas are available, extendable by application to the Public Security Bureau in China. Overstaying guarantees a fine of 500 *yuan* per day and delays at the airport.

Pharmacies

Take your own prescription drugs and a supply of minor medicaments. Non-prescription drugs, tampons and contraceptives may be available in the shopping centres of major hotels.

There is always a 24-hour pharmacy in big cities. For more serious problems, ask your hotel or guide for assistance with a doctor's visit, or a trip to the local hospital.

It is possible to find Internet connections in big cities

Post

Main post offices are open 8am–6pm and are easy to spot, with a dark green sign stating 'China Post' in English. Offices can be found on just about every major city road and they all offer a wide range of (often inefficient) postal services.

Public holidays

1 January	New Year
Late January/ early February	Chinese New Year (2/3-day holiday)
8 March	Women's Day
1 May	Labour Day
4 May	Youth Day
1 June	Children's Day
1 July	Communist Party Day
1 August	People's Liberation Army Day
1 October	National Day

Smoking

Smoking is socially acceptable almost everywhere. Some long-distance air-conditioned buses do try to stop smoking on board, often with little success. Airports are also supposed to be smoke free, but rarely is this enforced.

Suggested reading and media

The English-language newspaper *China Daily* is mainly filled with favourable 'news' about how well China is solving its problems. The *Shanghai Daily* and the weekly *Shanghai Star* are better.

All major foreign newspapers and magazines are available in Shanghai and other major cities. English-language entertainment publications contain current listings and are available free in bars, restaurants and hotels in all big cities. Titles include *City Weekend* and *That's Shanghai*.

Sustainable tourism

Thomas Cook is a strong advocate of ethical and fairly traded tourism and believes that the travel experience should be as good for the places visited as it is for the people who visit them. That's why we firmly support The Travel Foundation, a charity that develops solutions to help improve and protect holiday destinations, their environment, traditions and culture. To find out what you can do to make a positive difference to the places you travel to and the people who live there, please visit *www.thetravelfoundation.org.uk*

Tax

Top-end hotels usually, but by no means always, levy a 15 per cent service charge.

Telephones
Calling home from China

Australia: *00 + 61 + area code*
New Zealand: *00 + 64 + area code*
Republic of Ireland: *00 + 353 + area code*
South Africa: *00 + 27 + area code*

CONVERSION TABLE

FROM	TO	MULTIPLY BY
Inches	Centimetres	2.54
Feet	Metres	0.3048
Yards	Metres	0.9144
Miles	Kilometres	1.6090
Acres	Hectares	0.4047
Gallons	Litres	4.5460
Ounces	Grams	28.35
Pounds	Grams	453.60
Pounds	Kilograms	0.4536
Tons	Tonnes	1.0160

To convert back, for example from centimetres to inches, divide by the number in the third column.

UK: *00 + 44* + area code
USA and Canada: *00 + 1* + area code
NB: omit initial *0* in area codes.

Calling China from abroad
Dial the access code *00* from the UK, Ireland and New Zealand, *011* from the USA and Canada, and *0011* from Australia, followed by the country code for China (*86*) and the area code without the first *0.*

Mobile phones
China uses the European GSM mobile telephone system, although the American CDMA system is making inroads.

You can either bring your own phone or buy an inexpensive one in China and insert a prepaid SIM card to receive calls from abroad. If you're travelling about, make sure your SIM card is valid in all provinces – the cheapest ones are valid within a certain city or province only.

Time zone
All of China uses Beijing's time zone, GMT+8 hours, which makes for dark mornings in the far west. This puts Shanghai 8 hours ahead of London, 13 hours ahead of New York, 2 behind Melbourne and 4 behind New Zealand.

Toilets
Except in tourist areas, public pay toilets are not very pleasant, and squatting in public over an open sluice is fairly common. It is wise to take your own toilet paper. Toilets in the bigger hotels and restaurants are usually good.

Travellers with disabilities
Lack of facilities, difficulty of access, and overloaded transport make life hard for those with mobility problems. For further information, contact:

UK
Royal Association for Disability and Rehabilitation (RADAR)
12 City Forum, 250 City Road, London EC1V 8AF.
Tel: (020) 7250 3222.

USA
Society for Accessible Travel & Hospitality
347 Fifth Avenue, Suite 605, New York, NY 10016.
Tel: (212) 447 7284.

Language

China's principal language is Putonghua or 'common speech', better known as Mandarin in the western world. A number of quite different languages and dialects are spoken in the south; with the exception of Yunnanese Mandarin, all are quite unintelligible to each other as well as to Mandarin-speaking northerners. Since 1949, however, Putonghua – really Beijing Mandarin – has been the universal language of education and the media, so is understood and spoken (albeit sometimes reluctantly) throughout Southern China.

PRONUNCIATION

c	ts as in cats
q	ch
x	sh
z	dz as in kids
zh	j

TRANSPORT

airplane	fei ji
airport	fei ji chang
bus	gong gong qi che
bus station	gong gong qi che zhan
train	huo che
railway station	huo che zhan
car	qi che
taxi	chu zu qi che
bicycle	xi xing che

NUMBERS

1	yi
2	er
3	san
4	si
5	wu
6	liu
7	qi
8	ba
9	jiu
10	shi
20	ershi
30	sanshi
40	sishi
50	wushi
100	yibai
1,000	yiqian

FOOD AND DRINK

bread	mainba o
rice	fan
fried rice	chao fan
noodles	mian tiao
egg	ji dan
fish	yu
duck	ya zi
chicken	ji
beef	niu rou
pork	zhu rou
shrimp	xia mi
soup	tang
fruit	guo zi
plain water	kai shui
tea	cha
coffee	ka fei

WEEKDAYS

Monday	xing qi yi
Tuesday	xing qi er
Wednesday	xing qi san
Thursday	xing qi si
Friday	xing qi wu
Saturday	xing qi liu
Sunday	xing qi tian

ACCOMMODATION

Hotel	Fan dian
Guesthouse	Bing guan
Do you have a room?	Ni you bu you fang jian?
How much is it?	Duo shao qian?
Toilet	Ce suo

GENERAL PHRASES

Hello	Ni hao
Goodbye	Zai jian
How are you?	Ni hao ma?
I'm fine	Wo hen hao
Thank you	Xie xie ni
Please	Qing
Please help me	Qing bang wo mang
Excuse me	Lao jia
I am sorry	Duibuqi
When?	Shen me shi hou?
What is this?	Zhei shi shen mo?
I understand	Wo dong
I don't understand	Wo bu dong
Do you understand?	Ni dong bu dong?
Yes	Shi
No	Bu shi
I like ...	Wo xihuan ...
I don't like ...	Wo bu xihuan ...
Too expensive	Tai gui
Inexpensive	Bu gui pian yi
I would like to go to ...	Wo yao qu ...
Where is the ...?	Zai nar ...?
I would like a ticket	Wo yao mai piao
Straight ahead	Yi zhi zou
Left	Zuo bian
Right	You bian
Today	Jin tian
Yesterday	Ming tian
Tomorrow	Zuo tian

Emergencies

Emergency telephone numbers
Police *110*
Fire *119*
Accidents/ambulance *120*

These numbers are valid throughout China, but outside of Shanghai there may not be anyone who speaks English immediately available.

Medical services
Casualty
Medical treatment for foreigners in China is not free and can sometimes be expensive. Before receiving treatment at any hospital you should try to contact your insurer to check that you are fully covered. Always make sure that your travel insurance documents are with you at all times, as hospitals will need to see these before dispensing any treatment. The main hospitals in southern China are:

Huashan Hospital. *Foreigners' Ward 19th floor, 12 Wulumuqi Zhong. Tel: (021) 6248 9999 ext 1900.*
Shanghai United Family Hospital. *1139 Xian Xia, Changning District. Tel: (021) 5133 1900; 24-hour emergency hotline (021) 5133 1999.*

Doctors
China has some of the best doctors in the world pursuing both Chinese traditional medicine and Western practices. Most major cities have private hospitals and clinics with English-speaking doctors. Some of the larger pharmacies have a doctor on their staff.

Health and insurance
It is recommended that travellers keep tetanus and polio vaccinations up to date, and be vaccinated against typhoid and hepatitis A. Precautions against malaria should be taken by those travelling to rural areas or making river trips. Observe food and water hygiene precautions: drink bottled water, and ensure that food is cleanly prepared.

Be sure to take out comprehensive travel insurance before you travel to China.

Opticians
In the larger cities there are some excellent opticians, many of whom speak English. Prescription lenses with fashionable frames are available at prices well below what you would find in the West. Cheap reading glasses are available in many shops.

Safety and crime
Overall, tourists are unlikely to be affected by violent crime in China. More common are scams designed to separate you from your money, usually practised by touts pretending to be students. While the Chinese are friendly towards foreigners and you need not isolate yourself from such harmless contacts, do not allow yourself to be taken to buy anything, or go a restaurant or bar with anyone you

meet on the street. This is a standard *modus operandi* of con artists in China, and your new friend might leave you with a grossly inflated bill to pay.

Pickpocketing and bag slicing occurs, but can be avoided with a few sensible precautions such as carrying only the money you need with you in a front trouser pocket. Make a photocopy of your passport, and leave the original in your hotel with other valuables. Be especially careful in markets and train stations. City streets are safe and relaxed at night.

Prostitution, although illegal, flourishes in the big cities, and carries the same inherent dangers as anywhere else in the world.

Lost property

Airports, railway stations and the more important bus depots all have lost-property offices. You should report loss of goods to the police.

Embassies and consulates

Foreign embassies in China

Australia

1168 West Nanjing Road.
Tel: (021) 5292 5500.

Canada

1376 West Nanjing Road, Suite 604.
Tel: (021) 6279 840.

Ireland

3 Ritan Dong, Beijing 100600.
Tel: (010) 6532 2691.

New Zealand

989 Changle.
Tel: (021) 5407 5858.

UK

1376 West Nanjing Road, Suite 301.
Tel: (021) 6279 7650.

USA

1038 West Nanjing Road.
Tel: (021) 3217 4650.

Chinese embassies abroad:

Australia

15 Coronation Drive, Yarralumla, Canberra. Tel: (02) 6273 4783.

Canada

515 St Patrick Street, Ottawa, Ontario K1N 5H3. Tel: (613) 789 3434.

Ireland

40 Ailesbury Road, Dublin 4.
Tel: (1) 269 1707.

New Zealand

2–6 Glenmore Street, Kelburn, Wellington. Tel: (04) 472 1382.

UK

49–51 Portland Place, London W1B 1JL.
Tel: (020) 7299 8428.

USA

2300 Connecticut Avenue NW, Washington, DC 20008.
Tel: (202) 328 2500.

Police

Officers wear green uniforms with peaked caps. They are generally helpful to foreigners, but this may be made difficult by the language barrier. In Shanghai, the Foreign Affairs Branch of the local PSB (*333 Wusong. Tel: (021) 6357 7925*) is staffed with officials who speak English.

Directory

Accommodation price guide

The accommodation prices are based on the cost per person for two people sharing the least expensive double room with en suite bathroom and including breakfast.

★	Under 500RMB
★★	500–1,000RMB
★★★	1,001–1,500RMB
★★★★	Above 1,500RMB

Eating out price guide

Price ranges are per person for a three-course meal without drinks.

★	Under 40RMB
★★	40–80RMB
★★★	81–150RMB
★★★★	Above 150RMB

SHANGHAI

ACCOMMODATION

East Asia Hotel ★
Shanghai has very few good budget accommodation options, but the East Asia Hotel is one of them. Established back in the 1930s, it's always busy and the bars and restaurants are popular with locals. Rooms are modest, but clean and comfortable. Centrally located for shopping.
680 Nanjing.
Tel: (021) 6322 3223.
Fax: (021) 6322 4598.
Metro: Renmin Gongyuan.

Astor House Hotel ★★
Established in 1846 during the Qing Dynasty, this hotel is steeped in history. Recently rescued by a renovation, the Astor still has that old-world charm. Standard rooms are very economical, but elegant Victorian suites in hardwood décor are also available. Full of atmosphere and a great location on the Bund.
15 Huangpu,
Huangpu District.
Tel: (021) 6324 6388.
Fax: 6324 3179.
sales@pujianghotel.com.
www.pujianghotel.com.
Metro: Henan Zhong Lu.

Park Hotel ★★
When this hotel was built in 1934, it was the tallest building in Asia. Art deco architecture sets the tone. The Park is not the most sophisticated of hotels but distinguished nonetheless. Overlooks People's Park and boasts Chinese and Western restaurants, a nightclub and a shopping arcade.
170 Nanjing Xi.
Tel: (021) 6327 5225.
Fax: (021) 6327 6958.
parkhtl@parkhotel.com.cn.
www.parkhotel.com.cn.
Metro: Renmin Gongyuan.

Gu Xiang Dajiudian (Howard Johnson Plaza Hotel) ★★★
Within easy walking distance of the Bund and just off the Nanjing Road pedestrian walkway, this 27-storey tower is decidedly more upmarket

than any Howard Johnson you might find in the USA. Facilities include one of Shanghai's best-equipped gyms.
595 Jiujiang,
Huangpu District.
Tel: (021) 3313 4888.
Fax: (021) 3313 4880.
reservations.shanghai@
hojoplaza.com.
www.hojoshanghai.com.
Metro: Renmin
Guangchang or Henan
Zhong Lu.

Heping Fandian (Peace Hotel) ★★★
One of Shanghai's most famous landmarks, the Peace Hotel, originally the Cathay Hotel, first opened its doors in 1929. The Sassoon family, an Iraqi Jewish clan, were the original owners. The Peace is especially connected with Victor Sassoon, who made his fortune in opium trading in Bombay and then settled into a life of excess in Shanghai. In the 1930s he was famous for his fancy-dress parties that shocked even decadent Shanghai. Today, suites are the best option as most of the standard rooms are a bit small.

The art deco architecture is interesting and, even if you are not staying in the hotel, it's worth making a detour to visit this fascinating place.
20 Nanjing Dong,
Huangpu District.
Tel: (021) 6321 6888.
Fax: (021) 6329 0300.
sales@shanghaipeacehotel.com.
www.shanghaipeacehotel.com. Metro: Henan Zhong Lu.

Ramada Plaza ★★★
The lobby is somewhat dramatic and bright with its marble columns and Greek statues, but the suites are very tasteful, with dark woods and fine upholstery. Considerably more economical than other major hotels in the area.
700 Jiujiang,
Huangpu District.
Tel: (021) 6350 0000.
Fax: (021) 6350 8490.
www.ramadainternational.com.
Metro: Renmin Gongyuan.

Portman Ritz-Carlton ★★★★
Located centrally and surrounded by excellent restaurants and shopping

venues, the 50-storey Portman Ritz-Carlton is less exotic than other 5-star hotels in Shanghai, but excels in comfort and amenities. Excellent health and sports club with squash courts and an indoor pool.
1376 Nanjing Xi,
Jingan District.
Tel: (021) 6279 8888.
Fax: (021) 6279 8800.
www.ritzcarlton.com.
Metro: Jing'an Si.

Pudong Shangri-La ★★★★
Located on the east side of the river in Pudong, the city's financial centre, the Shangri-La offers outstanding views and luxury suites. There's also an excellent spa and health club for guests.
33 Fu Cheng, Pudong.
Tel: (021) 6882 8888.
Fax: (021) 6882 6688.
slpu@shangri-la.com.
www.shangri-la.com.
Metro: Lujiazui.

Shanghai Siji Jiudian (Four Seasons Hotel) ★★★★
A classically elegant place in the best traditions of the Four Seasons Group. With the palm trees and a fountain in the marble-

lined lobby, you would never know that busy Nanjing Road was so close. The rooms are large and classic. With a jazz club on the top floor and one of the best Cantonese restaurants in Shanghai, the facilities are second to none.
500 Weihai, Jingan District.
Tel: (021) 6256 8888.
Fax: (021) 6256 5678.
www.fourseasons.com.
Metro: Shimen Yi Lu.

Westin Bund Center ★★★★
This majestic 50-storey hotel is located close to the Bund and within a stone's throw of the city's shopping and nightlife districts. Popular with business people, its restaurants offer a variety of international cuisine. Rooms are modern and tastefully decorated; the service impeccable.
88 Yan'an Henan, Huangpu District.
Tel: (021) 6335 1888.
Fax: (021) 6335 2888.
rsvns-shanghai@ westin.com. www. westin.com/shanghai.
Metro: Henan Zhong Lu.

EATING OUT

Grape ★
Cheap and cheerful, this bustling little eatery is a firm favourite of locals and expats alike. Try the sweet and sour pork, lemon chicken, garlic shrimp and bean curd.
55 Xinle, Luwan District, close to Xiangyang Market.
Tel: (021) 5404 0486.
Open: 10am–2am.
Metro: Huangpi Nan.

Lulu Restaurant ★★
The original Lulu's is still situated across the river in Pudong, but this newer location serves up better Shanghai dishes in a trendier atmosphere. Hairy crab is a must, as are the pork meatballs. Great place for a group night out.
5/F Plaza 66, 1266 Nanjing Xi.
Tel: (021) 6288 1179.
Open: 11am–2.30pm & 5–11pm. Metro: Dongchang Lu.

Da Marco ★★★
The best Italian in Shanghai is Da Marco. If you are in the mood for authentic pizza, lasagne, Caprese salad and fine wine, then this

is your place. Also serves up an excellent set lunch. Centrally located.
62 Yandang, Luwan District. Tel: (021) 6385 5998. Open: Noon–11pm. Metro: Huangpi Nan Lu.

Haishang Ashu (Shanghai Uncle) ★★★
An interesting recent addition to Shanghai's burgeoning dining scene, Shanghai Uncle was opened by Clarence Lee, a Shanghainese-American and son of a former *New York Times* food critic. In addition to the house speciality of crispy flamed pork, try the traditional Shanghai dish of cold smoked fish. The Peking pancakes with scallops and XO sauce are also of the highest order. It's wise to make a reservation.
222 Yan'an Dong, near Henan Zhong.
Tel: (021) 6339 1977.
Open: 11am–11pm.
Metro: Henan Zhong Lu.

La Seine ★★★
You might be taken aback by the Chinese décor with deep purple suede and silks, but La Seine is still very much French cuisine. Dishes

are served in delicate portions, allowing you to sample several of the fine appetisers and entrées. Try the *foie gras*, *escargots*, tilapia in mustard-cream sauce and any of the fresh salads. Good selection of wines and delicious desserts. La Seine also hosts a small patisserie, so you can buy fresh bread, cakes and croissants.

8 Jinan, Luwan District. Tel: (021) 6384 3722. Open: 11.30am–2.30pm & 6–11pm. Metro: Huangpi Nan Lu.

1221 ★★★★

Popular with the city's high-society types, 1221 is classy and chic. Traditional Shanghainese cuisine served in a Parisian atmosphere. Try the chicken in green onion soy sauce, or the *shaguo shizi tou* (lion's head pork meatballs). Advance bookings essential.

1221 Yan'an Xi, Changning District. Tel (021) 6213 6585/2441. Open: 11.30am–2pm & 5–11pm. Metro: Zhongshan Gongyuan.

Jean Georges ★★★★

A fusion of French and Asian cuisines is on offer at this highly recommended restaurant devised by Jean-Georges Vongerichten, a native of the Alsace region of France and now famous the world over for a series of fabulously eclectic restaurants. Specialities include a highly original *foie gras brûlé* and a mouth-watering lamb loin with black trumpet mushrooms. For many, this is Shanghai's best Western restaurant. It's advisable to make a booking well in advance.

3 Zhongshan Yi Dong, 4th floor, 3 on the Bund. Tel: (021) 6321 7733. Open: 11.30am–2.30pm & 6pm–11pm. Metro: Henan Zhong Lu.

M on the Bund ★★★★

Top-quality Western cuisine served with one of the best views of the waterfront and the Pudong skyline. Serves good Mediterranean and Middle Eastern cuisine and has an excellent collection of wines. Try the salt-crusted leg of lamb and goose. Desserts are also delicious, especially pavlova. Make a reservation. Neat attire a must.

7/F 20 Guangdong, Huangpu District. Tel: (021) 6350 9988. Open: daily 11.30am–2.30pm & 6–10.30pm. Metro: Yan'an Henan.

ENTERTAINMENT

Attica

Attica, one of Shanghai's top clubs with a list of internationally famous DJs, is located on the top floor of a stylish old building on the Bund. With two separate dancing venues and a terrace that provides great views of the river and the Pudong skyline, this is certainly a place to see and be seen.

15 Zhongshan Er Dong, 11th floor, Huangpu District. Tel: (021) 6373 3588. Open: 6pm–2am. Metro: Henan Zhong Lu.

Bar Rouge

Regarded by many as Shanghai's most glamorous night-time

entertainment venue, Bar Rouge plays host to the city's super chic. Excellent views of Pudong, an extensive cocktail menu, and DJs from around the world serve to make this a memorable experience.

18 Zhongshan Yi Dong, 7th Floor, 18 on the Bund, Huangpu District. Tel: (021) 6339 1199. Open: 6.30pm–1.30am. Metro: Henan Zhong Lu.

Cloud 9 and Sky Lounge

Take three different elevators to get to what currently claims to be the world's highest bar in a man-made creation. Found on the 87th floor of the Grand Hyatt Hotel, Cloud 9 offers superb views of the Huangpu River and the Bund. The Sky Lounge is above Cloud 9 and offers a more intimate escape.

Jin Mao Tower, 88 Shiji Dadao, Pudong. Tel: (021) 5049 1234. Open: 6pm–1am. Metro: Lujiazui.

Cotton Club (Nightclub)

It's dark and smoky, but the Cotton Club is the place for live music, especially jazz or rhythm 'n' blues.

8 Fuxing Xi, Xuhui District. Tel: (021) 6437 7110. Open: daily 7.30pm–2.30am. Metro: Xujiahui.

DR Bar

The DR, a chic and stylish martini bar, is where Shanghai's beautiful people come to order their champagne and cocktails. The décor – marble walls, black leather sofas and polished silver bar top – creates a sense of tranquillity.

15 North Block, Taicang, Xintiandi. Tel: (021) 6311 0358. Open: 4pm–1am. Metro: Huangpi Nan Lu.

Face Bar

Situated in a villa in the beautiful gardens of the Ruijin Guesthouse in the French Concession, the Face's chic bar provides a relaxing opportunity to sit back and unwind after the rigours of this busy city.

Ruijin Guesthouse, 118 Ruijin Er, Luwan District. Tel: (021) 6466 4328. Open: noon–1.30am. Metro: Shanxi Nan Lu.

Monsoon Bar

Originally an art deco brewery overlooking Suzhou Creek, the Pier One complex was recently renovated, and a number of exclusive restaurants and bars opened their doors to the public. The Monsoon Bar offers an eclectic mix of dance music in a stylish rooftop location. Dining possibilities at the Monsoon include one of Shanghai's best brunches and intimate late-night supping.

Pier One, 82 Yichang. Tel (021) 5155 8311. Open: noon–1.30am. Metro: Zhenping Lu.

O'Malley's Irish Pub

This cosy bar, located in an old Shanghai mansion, has an elegant hardwood interior and Irish antiques. Guinness® on tap, of course, and live Irish fiddlers at weekends. O'Malley's is also an ideal place for enjoying a drink outdoors in warm weather. Popular for live sports on big-screen TV.

42 Taojiang, Xuhui

District. Tel: (021) 6474
4533. Metro: Xujiahui.
**Shanghai Centre
Theatre (Acrobatics)**
Home to the Shanghai
Acrobatic Troupe, this is
one of the city's prime
venues and most riveting
attractions. Similar to a
circus with fire-eaters,
trapeze artists, clowns
and jugglers. Great
family entertainment,
not to be missed. Tickets
available from venue.
*1376 Nanjing Xi, Jingan
District.*
Tel: (021) 6279 8663.
Open: 7.30pm onwards.
Metro: Jing'an Si.
**Shanghai Concert Hall
(Theatre and Music)**
For performances of
classical works, both
Western and Chinese.
Home of the Shanghai
Symphony Orchestra.
Tickets available from
venue.
*523 Yan'an Dong,
Luwan District.*
Tel: (021) 6386 9153.
Metro: Huangpi Nan Lu.
**Shanghai Dajuyuan
(Shanghai Grand
Theatre)**
Apart from the
occasional Chinese opera
show, Shanghai's premier
theatre venue hosts
Western opera, ballet and
musicals. It is the home
of the Shanghai
Broadcast Symphony
Orchestra and a number
of foreign classical
orchestras have
performed here.
*300 Renmin Dadao,
Renmin Guangchang.*
Tel: (021) 6387 5480.
*Metro: Renmin
Guangchang.*
**Yifu Dajuyuan
(Yifu Theatre)**
Certainly not to
everyone's liking,
Chinese opera is
definitely an acquired
taste. The music, using a
variety of stringed
instruments and gongs,
can seem dissonant and
jarring, and the plot will
be impenetrable to those
not fluent in Chinese.
Fortunately, however,
the acrobatic component
of any Chinese opera
needs no translation
and the costumes are
bright and attractive.
The Shanghai version,
known as *kunqu*,
differs slightly from
the Beijing variety,
as it uses woodwind
instruments rather
than stringed
instruments.
*701 Fuzhou, Renmin
Guangchang.*
Tel: (021) 6351 4668.
*Box office open:
9am–7.30pm. Metro:
Renmin Guangchang.*

SPORT AND LEISURE
**Banyan Tree Shanghai
(Spa)**
For the ultimate in
pampering, this luxury
spa offers everything
from massage and scrubs
to beauty care in holistic
and aromatic bliss.
*Westin Shanghai, Bund
Center, 88 Yan'an Henan.*
Tel: (021) 6335 1888.
*spa-shanghai@
banyantree.com.*
*www.banyantreespa.com/
shanghai.*
Metro: Yan'an Henan.
**Changning Tennis
Centre**
A good place to meet
keen amateurs and also
the odd professional.
Court fees are reasonable
and general facilities
excellent.
*Lane 1038, Huashan,
Changning District.*
Tel: (021) 6252 4436.
Open: 8am–9pm.
Metro: Jiangsu Lu.

Shanghai International Circuit (Motor Racing)

Shanghai is host to one of the last races of the Formula One season, usually in early October. If you are not there in October, there might still be a minor race.

Anting District.
Tel: (021) 6330 5555.
www.f1ticket.info

Shanghai International Golf and Country Club

Shanghai's top golf course was designed by Robert Trent Jones Jr. It is a beautiful course that includes a water hazard at almost every hole. Unfortunately, to play you must be a guest at the Sheraton Grand Tai Ping Hotel in Hongqiao, or be introduced by a member. You can get there by car or taxi.

961 Yin Zhu, Zhujiajiao, Qingpu County.
Tel: (021) 5972 8111.
Open: 9am–5pm.
Closed: Tue.

Tianma Country Club (Golf)

Shanghai has over 20 golf courses, but many are off-limits to non-members.

Tianma is welcoming and offers club rental and caddies. 18 holes with beautiful views of Sheshan Mountain.

3958 Zhaokun, Tianma Town, Songjiang District.
Tel: (021) 5766 1666.
Open: 6.30am–10pm.

SHANGHAI ENVIRONS

Hangzhou

Accommodation

Mingtown Youth Hostel ★

Hangzhou does have a Hyatt and a Shangri-La, but if you are looking for a friendly, family-run place, you can't beat the Mingtown. It's close to the lake and is popular with backpackers. Great atmosphere and a chance to organise camping, cycling or hiking tours. Internet access. Very modest, but clean rooms.

10–11 Nanshan.
Tel: (0571) 8791 8948.

Xihu State Guest Hotel ★★★

Also known as Liu's Vila, this was once the country estate of a local millionaire. Located on a scenic 6-hectare (15-acre) site on the west side of the lake, the hotel is rightfully proud of its gardens and landscape. It has a 2-km (1¼-mile) frontage along the lake, as well as an outdoor pool and a golf course. As the name implies, the hotel is now managed by the local government, so don't expect facilities of an international standard, but the atmosphere compensates.

7 Xishan.
Tel: (0571) 8797 9889.
Fax: (0571) 8797 2348.
sales@xisgh.com.
www.xisgh.com

Eating out

Louwailou Restaurant ★★

Established in 1938, this is probably Hangzhou's favourite diner. Immortal local recipes such as *sudong po* (pork) and beggar's chicken compete with West Lake specialities, *xihu cuyu* (sweet and sour carp) and Longjing shrimps. With a lovely view overlooking the lake, the Louwailou makes for a great lunch.

30 Gushan.
Tel: (0571) 8702 9023.
Open: 9am–10pm.
Peppino's ★★★
Hangzhou's finest
Italian restaurant
presents a remarkable
range of Italian
flavours and a wine
cellar unsurpassed in
Zhejiang Province.
A multitude of pastas,
wood-fired pizzas
and some excellent
fish and seafood
dishes.
Hangzhou Xiangelila
Fandian (Shangri-la
Hotel), 78 Beishan.
Tel: (0571) 8707 7951.
www.shangri-la.com.
Open: 5.30pm–11pm.

ENTERTAINMENT
Night and Day
(Nightclub)
Of all the bars and
clubs along Nanshan Lu
strip, this is the pick
of the bunch. Offers live
music, often Latino, in
the evenings and late-
night dancing. Fine
views from the top-floor
balcony overlooking
West Lake.
240 Nanshan.
Tel: (0571) 8777 0275.
Open: 10am–2am.

Moganshan
ACCOMMODATION
Moganshan Lodge ★
Located in the Songliang
Shanzhuang Hotel, the
Moganshan Lodge is
managed by a Chinese
lady whose British
husband is the chef.
They provide great
Western meals and
have a café and bar
with a good choice of
wines and spirits. The
English-speaking source
of information for all
things Moganshan.
Requires advance
bookings.
Songliang Shanzhuang,
Yin Shan.
Tel: (0572) 803 3011.
info@
moganshanlodge.com.
www.
moganshanlodge.com
Radisson Villas ★★★
This lush hillside retreat
has two magnificent
villas that have been
partitioned into suites.
One was the hideaway of
notorious Shanghai
gangster Du Yuesheng
and Chiang Kaishek. The
other belonged to a
Swedish missionary.
These splendid villas
make for a great weekend

getaway. Better known
locally as Leidisen
Moganshan Bieshu, the
villas are now managed
by the Radisson group
and you would be
advised to book in
advance via their
Hangzhou location.
Moganshan.
Tel: (0572) 803 3601.
hzrph1@mail.hz.zj.cn.
www.radisson.com.cn

Nanjing
ACCOMMODATION
Jinling Hotel ★★★
Centrally located first-
class hotel with excellent
rooms. Western and
Chinese restaurants,
including a revolving
restaurant on the 36th
floor. Modern,
comfortable suites, and
a sauna and gym for
guests.
2 Hanzhong.
Tel: (025) 471 1888.
nj.jinling@
jinlinghotel.com.
www.jinlinghotel.com
Sheraton Nanjing
Kingsley Hotel &
Towers ★★★★
Situated on the banks of
the Yangzi River, the
Sheraton offers spacious
rooms and impeccable

service. Although catering largely to business travellers, there's a good fitness centre, jogging path, and even a lively Irish pub.

169 Hanzhong.
Tel: (025) 8666 8888.
Fax: (025) 8666 9999.
nanjing.kingsley
@sheraton.com.
www.sheraton.com/
NanjingKingsley

EATING OUT
Sichuan Jiujia ★★
More than just spicy Sichuan dishes here. This modest eatery also serves up some of Nanjing's favourite recipes, such as *yanshui ya* (salted baked duck) which is tender and delicious.

171 Taiping Nan.
Tel: (025) 8460 8801.
Open: 11am–11pm.
Bella Napoli ★★★
Italian-owned restaurant offering authentic wood-fired pizza and a selection of fine pasta dishes. Extensive menu of Italian cuisine includes steaks and vegetarian options. Italian wines also available.

75 Zhongshan Dong.
Tel: (025) 8471 8397.
Open: Mon–Fri 11am–2pm & 5.30–10.30pm.
Sat–Sun 11.30am–11pm.
Golden Harvest Thai Opera Café (Jinhe Tai Canting) ★★★
Purports to serve authentic Thai cuisine, but many of the dishes bear a strong Chinese influence. Nevertheless, it does make a change from more traditional Chinese fare. The venue is popular with local expats and serves a number of spicy curries.

Hunan, 2 Shizi Qiao.
Tel: (025) 8324 1823.
Open: 10am–2.30pm & 5pm–10.30pm.

Putuoshan
ACCOMMODATION
Luyuan Holiday Inn ★★
Located near the Fayu Temple in the centre of Zhoushan Island, this quaint resort has spacious rooms with balconies overlooking the sea. Staff are particularly friendly. Spa, health club and tennis also available.

61 Fayu.

Tel: (0580) 669 0588.
Fax: (0580) 609 2537.
web@putuoshan.net

Suzhou
ACCOMMODATION
Bamboo Grove Hotel ★★
A pleasant resort in the centre of the city. The grounds and restaurant areas are done in Suzhou style and surround a rock pool that is home to ducks and fish. Rooms are comfortable and have all mod-cons. Usually live music in the foyer bar at night.

168 Zhuhui.
Tel: (0512) 6520 5601.
Fax: (0512) 6520 8778.
www.bg-hotel.com
Shangri-La ★★★★
Only opened in July 2006, but the Shangri-La is everything you would expect from a 5-star hotel. Elegant suites, first-class service and fine dining. The hotel also hosts some good nightlife with a ballroom and a popular nightclub, Club Red.

168 Ta Yuan.
Tel: (0512) 6808 0168.
Fax: (0512) 6808 1168.

slsz@shangri-la.com.
www.shangri-la.com

EATING OUT
**Pine and Crane
Restaurant** ★★
A local landmark
restaurant that has
served Suzhou
specialities such as
Squirrel Shaped
Mandarin Fish and
Gusu Marinated Duck
for 200 years. English
menu and tourist-savvy
staff.
141 Guanqian.
Tel: (0512) 6727 7006.
Open: 11.30am–1.30pm
& 5–8.30pm.
**Suzhou Snack
Restaurant** ★★
Famous for Suzhou's
local Wu cuisine, where
dishes tend to be slightly
sweeter and softer in
texture than in other
parts of the country.
Some of the more
famous items on the
menu are seasonal,
so do be prepared to
chop and change
your order depending on
availability of products.
19 Taijian Nong,
Guanqian.
Tel: (0512) 6523 7603.
Open: 8am–9pm.

**CHANG JIANG
Chongqing**
ACCOMMODATION
Harbour Plaza ★★
In a city relatively
unaccustomed to foreign
visitors, this hotel does
very well in creating an
international
atmosphere. The
Harbour Plaza is
relatively inexpensive,
but modern and
comfortable. Centrally
located.
Wu Yi, Yuzhong District.
Tel: (023) 6370 0888.
Fax: (023) 6370 0788.
hpcq@harbour-plaza.com
www.harbour-plaza.com/
hpcq

Wuhan
ACCOMMODATION
Xuangong Hotel ★★
A heritage building,
founded circa 1930, and
located in the bustling
centre of the city. An
old-worldly ambience
pervades. Try to secure a
room with a balcony
overlooking the
shopping street below.
Also boasts a decent
restaurant famed for the
blue-snout bream
Wuchang fish once
served to Chairman Mao.

57 Jianghan.
Tel: (027) 6882 2588.
Fax: (027) 6882 2598/9.
www.xuangonghotel.com

**THE SOUTHWEST
Chengdu**
ACCOMMODATION
Jinjiang Hotel ★★★
This enormous hotel is
recognised by locals as
the centre of the town. It
was the first of Chengdu's
luxury hotels and, as
such, has a historical
ambience. Also boasts a
piano bar and a rooftop
restaurant offering a
great view over the city.
80 Renmin Dadao.
Tel: (028) 8550 6666.
Fax: (028) 8550 6550.
www.jjhotel.com

EATING OUT
Huang Cheng Laoma ★★
When in Sichuan, do as
the Sichuanese do:
hotpot! Woks and
burners are fitted into
each table and the waiter
will heat up the oil in
your wok with loads of
chillis. Then you dip
meat, chicken and
vegetables into the
steaming broth,
fondue-style. Wash it
down with cold beer.

20 Nan Shan Duan.
Tel: (028) 8513 9999.
Open: 11am–11pm.

Long Chaoshou ★★
A veritable feast of traditional Chengdu snacks downstairs, with spicy Sichuan hotpot upstairs. One of the city's oldest and most famous restaurants, Long Chaoshou opened in 1940. Excellent sweets.
8 Chunxi Nan.
Tel: (028) 667 6345.
Open: 10am–9pm.

ENTERTAINMENT
Sichuan Opera Theatre
There are over 2,000 different Sichuan opera plays, many dating back 250 years. The high-pitched wailing of the music can be off-putting to some, but the speed of the 'face-changing' scenes will leave you breathless. Tickets available from the venue.
20 Zhuangyuan.
Tel: (028) 8665 8400.

Dali
ACCOMMODATION
Jim's Peace Hotel ★
A backpackers' favourite, Jim's rooms are basic but clean. The atmosphere is what makes the place. Chinese antiques, rattan seats and lots of people to meet. Jim's organise tours, bicycles and anything else you want. Internet access.
57 Bao Ai.
Tel: (0872) 267 9048.

Lan Lin Ge Fandian (Landscape Hotel) ★
This charming courtyard hotel incorporates a distinct Chinese architecture and local ethnic Bai designs. Pleasant courtyard garden to relax in or enjoy breakfast. Conveniently located in the heart of the ancient city.
96 Yu Er.
Tel: (0872) 266 6318.
Fax: (0872) 266 6189.

Kunming
ACCOMMODATION
Kunming Hotel ★★
The most popular place in town, and not just for tourists; locals love to hang out here too. The Kunming Hotel has one great restaurant called Chaozhou, bars, a disco and even a bowling alley.
52 Dongfeng Dong.
Tel: (0871) 316 2063.
www.
kunminghotel.com.cn

Greenland Hotel ★★★
Elegant and tastefully decorated suites with all mod-cons. The Greenland also has excellent restaurants and health and sports facilities. If you are wondering where the name comes from, it's the neon green lights that light up the hotel's exterior at night.
80 Tuodong.
Tel: (0871) 318 9999.
www. greenlandhotel. com.cn

EATING OUT
Wei's Pizzeria ★★
Here's a rare chance to try 'fusion' pizza. Wood-fired thin pizzas are served with tasty Yunnan treats such as *taoza rubbing* (fried goat's cheese and Yunnan ham). There's Indian food, too, so try a Chicken Masala Pizza if you can. Ice cold beers accompany this meal perfectly. Great atmosphere for locals and tourists alike.
27 Xiaodong.
Tel: (0871) 316 6189.
Open: 10.30am–10pm.

THE SOUTH
Guangzhou
ACCOMMODATION
Garden Hotel ★★★

Chic, perhaps even ostentatious, this hotel claims to have the largest lobby in Asia. With a total of 828 rooms and suites, the Garden Hotel is a high-rise palace. However, it is recognised as one of the top hotels in China and the main reasons are the facilities and the service, which is delightful but professional. There's a rooftop garden, tennis courts, squash, a pool and a number of good restaurants.
368 Huanshi Xi.
Tel: (020) 8333 8989.
Fax: (020) 8335 0467.
www.
thegardenhotel.com.cn

EATING OUT
Guangzhou Restaurant ★★

Established in 1939, this three-floor eatery is always bustling and noisy, but the food is great. Cantonese favourites such as dim sum and Wenchang chicken are just part of the extensive menu.

2 Wenchang Nan.
Tel: (020) 8138 0388.
Open: 7am–3pm &
5.30pm–10pm.

ENTERTAINMENT
Xinghai Concert Hall

Guangzhou's finest concert hall is famous for its near perfect acoustics. The Xinghai seats up to 1,500 patrons. *That's Guangzhou* magazine (*www.thatsguangzhou.com*) has weekly listings of times, dates and orchestras. Tickets available from venue.
33 Qingbo.
Tel: (020) 8735 2766/ 2222.

Guilin
ACCOMMODATION
Guilin Flowers Youth Hostel ★

A budget accommodation option for those who are looking for a family atmosphere and a centre for organising day trips. Bright and cosy with friendly staff, this is a home from home. However, some of the rooms are rather sparsely furnished.
6 Shangzhi, Zhongshan.
Tel: (0773) 383 9625.

Bravo Hotel ★★★★

Very reasonably priced 4-star hotel with all amenities, including Guilin's only swimming pool. Nicely located on the banks of Rong Lake. Sometimes very busy with tour groups. Reserve in advance.
14 Ronghu Nan.
Tel: (0773) 282 3950.
glbravo@sina.com.
www.guilinbravo.com

EATING OUT
Yiyuan Fandian ★★

Consistently excellent and serving some of the spiciest Sichuan dishes you'll ever be treated to, this restaurant is a 'must do' while staying in Guilin. Try the stir-fried chicken in chilli and garlic, the *shuizhu niurou* (tender beef and vegetables in chilli sauce), *tangcu cuipi yu* (crispy sweet 'n' sour fish) and, not to be forgotten, stir-fried eel with dried chillis and Sichuan spices.
Nanhuan.
Tel: (0773) 282 0470.
Open: 11.30am–2.30pm & 5.30–9.30pm.

Hainan Island

ACCOMMODATION

Gloria Resort Sanya ★★★

Located on a pristine beach in chic Yalong Bay, this is the modern Mediterranean-style hotel that most Westerners crave. Rooms are comfortable with white upholstery and rattan furnishings. French windows open out to balconies facing the sea. Offers a self-contained holiday with good restaurants, lovely pool, and health and beauty facilities. Advance reservations recommended.

Yalong Bay, Sanya.
Tel: (0898) 8856 8855.
Fax: (0898) 8856 8853.
www.gloriaresort.com

Crown Spa Resort ★★★★

Resembling a white castle, this top resort is located 15km (9 miles) east of Haikou town and sits right on the beach. The suites are tasteful and standard rooms have hardwood floors and light upholstery to suit the sunny weather. Prices vary greatly with seasons and advance reservations are a necessity.

1 Qiongshan, East Riverside Haikou.
Tel: (0898) 6596 6888.
www.crownsparesorthainan.com

SPORT AND LEISURE

Red Coral International Water Sports Club

Not too many opportunities abound in China for underwater activities, but Yalong Bay is definitely the premier location for scuba diving and snorkelling. Aquamarine waters, beautiful coral and tropical fish await you. Red Coral is a reputable company with good equipment and safety standards. Bookings through most hotels.

Sunny Sanya Family Inn.
29 Haiyun, Dadonghai, Sanya.
Tel: (0898) 8820 0128.
Fax: (0898) 8821 3481.
www.sunnysanya.com

Yangshuo

ACCOMMODATION

Paradise Yangshuo Resort ★★★

Splendid resort located on the banks of a lake and set in lush gardens. The wooden-floored suites are elegant. Reserve a high-floor room to secure the daylight and a beautiful view from your balcony.

116 Yi. Tel: (0773) 882 2109/881 6888.
Fax: (0773) 882 2106.
www.paradiseyangshuo.com

ENTERTAINMENT

Impressions Liu Sanjie (Theatre)

A jaw-dropping folk musical theatre, directed by moviemaker Zhang Yimou. It is performed by the Li River with a stunning backdrop of karst mountains and water. Simply spectacular and not to be missed! Ask anywhere in town for booking details.

Performances daily: 8–9pm.

HONG KONG AND MACAO

Hong Kong Island

ACCOMMODATION

Ice House ★★

Conveniently located in the heart of Central District, very near Lan

Kwai Fong, this trendy little hotel is reasonably priced and friendly. Apartment suites have kitchen facilities. Reserve in advance and request a higher floor for less noise and more light.
38 Ice House Street, Central.
Tel: (0852) 2836 7333.
www.icehouse.com.hk.
Metro: Central.

Central Park ★★★
Ideally located a short walk from Central and SoHo, this unpretentious hotel is good value. Suites are cosy, modern and decorated in pastel shades and beige for a cool, soothing effect.
263 Hollywood Road, Central. Tel: (0852) 2850 8899. Fax: (0852) 3472 8888. www. centralparkhotel.com.hk. Metro: Central.

Jia ★★★★
If you are feeling glamorous, then this red-carpet boutique hotel is the place to see and be seen. Post-modern and baroque architecture designed by French design guru Philippe Starck that simply oozes chic. The standard rooms are well fitted but very small. The atmosphere at Jia is the key: try Opia restaurant for the best in fine dining.
1–5 Irving Street, Causeway Bay.
Tel: (0852) 3196 9000.
Fax: (0852) 3196 9001.
www.jiahongkong.com.
Metro: Causeway Bay.

EATING OUT
Luk Yu Tearoom ★★
A Hong Kong legend, the Luk Yu serves a wide range of teas and dim sum in an atmospheric back-street restaurant. Prices are calculated by abacus.
24–26 Stanley Street, Central.
Tel: (0852) 2523 5463.
Open: 7am–10pm.
Metro: Central.

Jumbo Floating Restaurant ★★★
It's somewhat a staple day out for many tourists, but well worth the experience. This floating restaurant sits in Aberdeen Harbour and offers guests great evening views of the Hong Kong skyline. There's fine seafood and, on Sundays, a champagne buffet.
Shum Wan Pier, Wong Chuk Hang, Aberdeen.
Tel: (0852) 2553 9111.
Open: Mon–Sat 11am–11.30pm, Sun 7.30am–11.30pm.

M at the Fringe ★★★
When M at the Fringe opened its doors in 1989 it was regarded as something of a trendsetter; a totally independent restaurant serving the highest quality food from a number of different world cuisines, all under one roof. The mostly Mediterranean fare includes a number of excellent vegetarian dishes and the menu changes every 3 months.
1/F, 2 Lower Albert Road, Central.
Tel: (0852) 2877 4000.
www. m-restaurantgroup.com.
Open: Lunch Mon–Fri noon–2.30pm, closed Sat & Sun. Dinner daily 7pm–10.30pm.
Metro: Central.

ENTERTAINMENT
Club 64
Located in the heart of the island's busiest

entertainment area and named after the Tiananmen Square massacre in 1989, the 6 referring to the month of June and 4 to the day the massacre occurred. It's a friendly bar with an eclectic clientele. The happy hours are usually between 3pm and 9pm. *12–14 Wing Wah Lane, Lan Kwai Fong. Open: Mon–Thur 3pm–2am, Fri & Sat 3pm–4am, Sun 3pm–1am. Metro: Central.*

Disneyland

Fun for all the family with a Chinese twist. All the magic and rides and shows you would expect. Weekends are much busier and more expensive than weekdays. *Lantau Island. Tel: (0852) 1830 830. www. hongkongdisneyland.com*

Ocean Park

An excellent place to take the kids, Ocean Park is one of the great adventure and theme parks of the world and, unlike some other theme parks, the entrance fee is not too steep. Apart from the stomach-churning rides, there are also plenty of animals to see, including sharks, dolphins and two lovable giant pandas. *Wong Chuk Hang & Nam Long Shan (Aberdeen). Tel: (0852) 2552 0291. www.oceanpark.com.hk. Open: 10am–6.30pm (summer); 10am–11pm (winter). Bus: 629 from Admiralty metro station.*

Kowloon

ACCOMMODATION

New Kings Hotel ★★

Located just off Nathan Road and in an area that appears at first to be a little away from Hong Kong's premier sights, the New Kings is actually right next to the Yau Ma Tei metro station and offers great value considering you're in Hong Kong. The Temple Street Night Market with its great noodle shops and cheap clothes stalls runs close by. *473 Nathan Road, Yau Ma Tei. Tel: (0852) 2780 1281. Metro: Yau Ma Tei.*

Stanford Hillview ★★

Especially good value for money and a good location for restaurants and nightlife, this unpretentious hotel caters to those who would rather avoid the decadence of some Hong Kong establishments. Rooms are modest, but they all have broadband Internet. *Observatory Road on Knutsford Terrace, Tsim Sha Tsui. Tel: (0852) 2722 7822. Fax: (0852) 2723 3718. hillview@ stanfordhotel.com. www.stanfordhillview.com. Metro: Tsim Sha Tsui.*

Peninsula ★★★★

One of the world's grandest hotels, the Peninsula is classical and colonial and yet still ultra-chic. From the fleet of Rolls-Royce Phantoms at the disposal of guests to the butler service and exquisite décor, a stay at the Peninsula is the holiday of a lifetime. *Salisbury Road. Tel: (0852) 2920 2888. Fax: (0852) 2722 4170. phk@peninsula.com. www.peninsula.com. Metro: Tsim Sha Tsui.*

EATING OUT
Gaylord ★★★
Of Hong Kong's many good Indian restaurants, Gaylord is the pick of the bunch. A classical touch and sumptuous spicy curries, plus live Indian music every night. Good selection of vegetarian dishes.
1st Floor, Ashley Centre, 23–25 Ashley Road, Tsim Sha Tsui.
Tel: (0852) 2376 1001.
Open: noon–3pm & 6–11pm. Metro: Tsim Sha Tsui.

Fook Lam Moon ★★★★
This restaurant likes to think it serves the best Cantonese cuisine in Hong Kong, quite a boast, but it is very good. The menu offers an endless list of dim sum dishes alongside some exotic sea creatures. How about steamed sea cucumber stuffed with minced shrimp or braised whole abalone with goose web and vegetables?
8 Luna Court, 53–59 Kimberley Road, Tsim Sha Tsui.
Tel: (0852) 2366 0286.
www. fooklammoon-grp.com.

Open: Mon–Sat 11.30am–3pm & 6pm–11pm, Sun 11am–3pm & 6pm–11pm.
Metro: Tsim Sha Tsui.

Macao
ACCOMMODATION
Grand Emperor ★★★
From the beefeaters at the door and the life-size portrait of Queen Elizabeth to the tuxedo-wearing guests, you might feel as though you have just walked into a James Bond film. However, the old-world charm works at this historical casino-hotel. Service is impeccable. Avoid Saturdays if possible as prices treble with the influx of casino aficionados.
288 Avenida Comercial de Macau.
Tel: (0853) 2888 9988.
Fax: (0853) 2888 9933.
sales@grandemperor.com
www.grandemperor.com

EATING OUT
Restaurante Fernando ★★★
Located on the promenade, Fernando is the perfect spot for

a lazy lunch. Try the seafood, done in Fernando's own Portuguese-Macanese style.
9 Praia de Hac Sa, Coloane.
Tel: (0853) 882 531/ 882 264. www.fernando-restaurant.com
Open: noon–9.30pm.

ENTERTAINMENT
Hotel Lisboa (Casino)
The biggest and most famous casino in Macao attracts high-rollers and casual tourists. Also offers nightly shows, restaurants and bars.
Avenida da Amizade.
Tel: (0853) 577 666.

The Venetian (Casino)
One of the new wave of Las Vegas-style casinos that have opened in the last ten years, The Venetian is more than just a casino; it offers sports events, rock concerts, theatre, hi-society shopping, over 30 restaurants... you name it! And of course, it's an exclusive resort-hotel too.
Taipa Island.
www.venetianmacao.com

Index

Acknowledgements

Thomas Cook wishes to thank the following libraries and associations for their pictures:

AA PHOTO LIBRARY Rick Strange 19, 30, 31, 63, 69, 75, 83, 86, 87, 97, 98, 99, 100, 102, 103, 109, 119, 121, 142, 145, 151

DREAMSTIME L Hui (1), A Yakovlev (5), L Fernanda (34, 139), M Poli (71), F Hui (80), Gary718 (91), B Benoit (92), Bayon (93), C Gonsalves (101), Kiankhoon (111), J Van Ostaeyen (125), T Craig (137), R Shader (138)

WORLD PICTURES PHOTOSHOT 35

The remaining pictures were taken by CPA Media / David Henley

For CAMBRIDGE PUBLISHING MANAGEMENT LTD:
Project editor: Diane Teillol
Typesetter: Julie Crane
Copy editor: Anne McGregor
Proofreader: Karolin Thomas
Indexer: Marie Lorimer

SEND YOUR THOUGHTS TO
BOOKS@THOMASCOOK.COM

We're committed to providing the very best up-to-date information in our travel guides and constantly strive to make them as useful as they can be. You can help us to improve future editions by letting us have your feedback. If you've made a wonderful discovery on your travels that we don't already feature, if you'd like to inform us about recent changes to anything that we do include, or if you simply want to let us know your thoughts about this guidebook and how we can make it even better – we'd love to hear from you.

Send us ideas, discoveries and recommendations today and then look out for your valuable input in the next edition of this title.

Emails to the above address, or letters to Travellers Series Editor, Thomas Cook Publishing, PO Box 227, Unit 9, Coningsby Road, Peterborough PE3 8SB, UK.

Please don't forget to let us know which title your feedback refers to!